The Sicilian Gentleman's
Cookbook

The Sicilian Gentleman's Cookbook

DON BARATTA

ILLUSTRATIONS BY GEORGE WALKER

FIREFLY BOOKS

A FIREFLY BOOK

Published by Firefly Books Ltd. 2002

First Printing 2002

Publisher Cataloging-in-Publication Data (U.S)

Baratta, Don, 1932-.
  The Sicilian gentleman's cookbook / Don Baratta ;
illustrations by George Walker. —Rev. ed.
 [276] p. : col. ill. ; cm.
Originally published by Rocklin, CA: Prima, 1992, rev. 1993.
Includes index.
Summary: A guide to the Sicilian and Sicilian-American food.
Includes over 160 recipes, 100 illustrations, anecdotes
and folklore.
ISBN 1-55209-632-7 (pbk.)
1. Cookery, Italian — Sicilian style.   2. Cookery — Italy.
I. Walker, George. II. Title.
641.5945 / 8 21   CIP   TX723.2S55B37 2002

**National Library of Canada Cataloguing
in Publication Data**

Baratta, Don, 1932-
            The Sicilian gentleman's cookbook

3rd rev. ed.
Includes index.
ISBN 1-55209-632-7

            1. Cookery, Italian—Sicilian style. I. Title.

TX723.2.S55B37 2002   641.59458   C2001-930725-X

Published in the U.S. in 2002 by
Firefly Books (U.S.) Inc.
P.O. Box 1338, Ellicott Station
Buffalo, New York 14205

Published in Canada in 2002 by
Firefly Books Ltd.
3680 Victoria Park Avenue
Willowdale, Ontario M2H 3K1

Illustrations, cover and design by George Walker

Printed and bound in Canada by
Gandalf
Toronto, Ontario

Printed on Appleton coated, Utopia Two,
text ivory matte #70 acid-free paper
Typeset in Adobe Garamond, Gill Sans, Tekton and Centaur.

*The Publisher acknowledges the financial support of the Government of
Canada through the Book Publishing Industry Development Program for
its publishing activities.*

Contents

 # *Attend!*

I shall explain this thing about Sicilians. You will scarcely believe it. In my father's house, as true of most Sicilians, a decent respect for food was not expected—it was required. I do not mean our family worshipped like some primitive tribe at a shrine. We were not heathens. But the Old Man was fond of pointing out (with obvious approval) that all religions started by offering a supreme being something to eat.

The Old Man was often annoyed that most Italian cookbooks were written by northern Italians. This, he said, gave a lopsided and inaccurate impression of Italian cuisine. To balance that impression, he compiled a list of recipes for foods he was in the habit of cooking throughout his long life.

Not, the Old Man asserted, that there is anything wrong with northern Italians or their cooking. They were all light-hearted, fun-loving citizens who seemed to be well-nourished and very nice people. Still, they did prefer Parmigiano cheese to the more strident Pecorino. They often as not used butter in place of olive oil. They were (with the possible exception of the Genoese) inordinately fond of pork. And they stuffed pasta with potato to create a dumpling that could be mistaken for something German.

Also, they ate corn!*

Here, then, is the Old Man's book of recipes. If you cannot get the exact "Sicilian" taste by following them, it may be because the Old Man flavored his meals with his personality as much as with his herbs and spices. On the other hand, perhaps he lied.

---

* *Mangiapolenta* (cornmeal eater): A common epithet used by Sicilians to describe nearly any Italian north of Rome; a reference to their eating habits, similar to the association of Frenchmen with frogs or Samuel Johnson's remark about Scotsmen and their oats. Nowadays, when we wish to be insulting, we refer to a person's politics, which is hardly a personal matter. The old ways are the best ways.

Antipasto and Salads

Antipasti e Insalate

 **BRING YOU RECIPES** from an obscure and ancient land. Some are very old. In those days the taste of food was limited only to what poor and simple herbs the countryside provided. How different now!

Regard the wonders of this new land. In the most ordinary of markets you will find a selection of herbs and spices that would have dazzled the eyes of a gourmet chef only a century ago. And all at the disposal of the most innocent of young cooks! Is it any wonder that this princely place is known as the Land of Opportunity? For myself, an Italian kitchen with American conveniences ... I could ask for little more. And still, there are fools who insist they see no positive progress in the human race.

Basta! Let them return to their caves and brood upon the calamities produced by cooking over an open fire.

But perhaps you would be happier if I got at once to the subject at hand.

Antipasto usually comes before the meal. However, for people living in warmer climes it can often take the place of a hot meal. And why not? The essence of living well is to indulge your whims. If it pleases you to consume antipasto at any time of the day for any reason, who is to deny you? A purist may be outraged, but happily neither you nor I am a purist.

For the same reason, salads are included here—though most Italians eat salads after the main course. Of course, this book is about Sicilian recipes, and being Sicilian is not the same thing as being Italian.*

---

* I have personally met many Italians who are not Sicilians, and every single one of them agreed wholeheartedly with my father about this difference. I have never been sure whether they or my father was more pleased with the distinction.

Salad Dressing
CONDIMENTO PER L'INSALATA

Here is a very simple dressing that will do you no harm.

You will need:

1 cup	extra virgin olive oil		¼ tsp	garlic salt
⅓ cup	red wine vinegar		¼ tsp	onion salt
2 tsp	chopped fresh oregano (or 1 tsp dried)		½ tsp	freshly ground black pepper
1 tsp	chopped fresh tarragon (or ½ tsp dried)			

Preparation:

Combine all ingredients in a pint jar. Shake vigorously until dressing emulsifies. (By the way, be sure the cover is on the jar when you shake it.)

Note: If fresh herbs are used, refrigerate the dressing. The dressing will "set," so bring it to room temperature before using, and it will return to its liquid state.

Yields 1½ cups.

Antipasto
ANTIPASTI

There are dozens of ways to build an antipasto tray, and all of them are messy and involve a great clatter of dishes. I recommend the following method. It eliminates the use of the conventional tray and brings the guests into direct contact with their food.

You will need:

well-rounded fresh lettuce leaves,
    1 per person
celery stalks (the center ones),
    1 per person
roasted red peppers cut into strips,
    2 strips per person
Italian dry salami, cut into sticks,
    1 per person (if bought presliced, 2–3
    slices per person)

capocollo (or spiced ham), cut into
    sticks, 1 per person (if bought
    presliced, 2–3 slices per person)

provolone cheese, cut into sticks,
    2 sticks per person
black and green pitted olives,
    2 per person
tuna, anchovies, or sardines,
    1 can per 3 people (optional)
Salad Dressing (optional)
    (see page 11)

Preparation:

Use a large round serving plate and place upon it as many lettuce leaves as you have guests. The leaves should be rounded to form cups.

Start by placing a celery stalk in the center of each leaf and then, for color contrast, the red pepper strips. Use your imagination in arranging the rest of the ingredients. When it's time to serve the antipasto, let each guest pick up a loaded leaf. You'll need to provide small plates if anyone wants to pour salad dressing over the thing.

Note: Many vegetables, such as artichokes and zucchini, are used in an antipasto. You may wish to browse through the chapter on vegetables.

Hot Dip, Sicilian Style
Bagno Caldo alla Siciliana

Bagno caldo means "warm bath" and refers to serving this dish hot. In all accuracy, I must point out that this sauce originated in Piedmont (Italy), where it is called *bagna cauda* and means the same thing as the more pronounceable Sicilian term. I include this recipe here because I like it.

In the north they make it with olive oil and butter. They also might add such ingredients as capers or fresh basil, and I certainly would have no argument with this. The Sicilian variation keeps the recipe simpler and adds fresh lemon juice in place of butter.

You will need:

4 tbsp	extra virgin olive oil		juice of 1 lemon
3	cloves garlic, minced	4 tbsp	wine vinegar (red or white)
2	green onions (white part only), minced	½ tsp	Tabasco sauce
		2 tsp	roasted red pepper, minced
salt and pepper to taste		vegetables for dipping	
1 can	(2 oz) anchovy fillets, drained		

Preparation:

Heat olive oil in a medium-size skillet and sauté the garlic and onions, along with the salt and pepper, until the garlic turns golden. Add anchovies and blend in with a fork. Add all the other ingredients and simmer slowly for a few minutes.

Pour sauce into a chafing dish (candle, alcohol, or electric) and keep sauce warm without letting it boil. The vegetables used should be as fresh as possible.

Yields about 1 cup.

Note: Cabbage, fennel, and artichokes should be steamed or blanched first, but others, like cucumbers, zucchini, bell peppers, turnips, or celery, can be eaten raw. All are delightful when dipped.

Eggplant Appetizer
CAPONATINA

Caponata, or its diminutive, caponatina, is a relish made from eggplant. Generally it is served cold, but I have seen it used hot as a filling between two slices of bread. I refer, of course, to the doughnut-shaped Sicilian loaves baked with sesame seeds on top.

As a boy home from school, I would often tear a piece from this bread, pour olive oil on top, and flavor it with salt and pepper. Sometimes I would heat it in the oven, but more often than not I would eat it as it was, stamping my feet in enjoyment as I went out to play. I'd heard that some people spread butter on bread instead of oil, but I considered that a matter for amusement rather than disdain.

I do not mean I never tasted soft, white, packaged bread. Our family was considered quite modern, even progressive, from the standpoint of the community, and on special occasions my mother would send me to buy a loaf. To be fair, I must admit to enjoying it, for I always ate a few slices on the way home. Since I'm bothering to be fair, I should also mention that I mistook it for a kind of cake.

But enough foolishness. Let us get on to something serious, like caponatina.

You will need:

2	medium eggplants	3 tbsp	sugar
salt		4 tbsp	red wine vinegar
½ cup	extra virgin olive oil	½ cup	thick tomato sauce
I	onion, finely chopped	¼ cup	small green olives, pitted
3	stalks celery, thinly sliced	½ cup	capers, drained
½ cup	dry white wine	salt and pepper to taste	

Preparation:

Peel eggplant and slice into ½″ slices. Place slices into a colander, salting each one and piling them one on top of the other. Cover with a saucer, and place a weight on top so the slices are under pressure. Allow at least an hour for the bitter juices to drain off.

Remove and run water over each slice, then pat dry. Now cut the slices into ½″ cubes and set them aside.

Use a large skillet and bring oil to high heat. Fry eggplant quickly to brown lightly on all sides. Remove and drain on paper towels.

Sauté the onion and celery in a skillet for 10 minutes. Pour in wine and stir until it has nearly evaporated. Return eggplant to pan.

Dissolve sugar in vinegar and pour over the eggplant mixture. Add tomato sauce, olives, and capers. Stir and blend in salt and pepper. Simmer slowly, allowing mixture to heat through. Remove from heat and let cool.

Serve cold as a relish, as a dip, or—for that matter—as anything you like.

Yields about 3 cups.

SHOULD YOU COME from an Italian family, you must be familiar with the habit of rubbing the cut tip of the zucchini or cucumber against the sliced end of the vegetable before peeling it. This, as all intelligent Italian housewives know, was said to draw out the poison from the vegetable and make it safe to eat. My mother did the same thing with eggplant—not a common practice, but she was considered somewhat conservative even for a Sicilian, and would not take chances in such affairs.

For those interested in history, lemon juice mixed with olive oil is a relic of the old Greek influence on our eating habits. For that matter, one would be hard put to find a nation that has not influenced our dishes. Everyone seems to have colonized or conquered Sicily at one time or another. However, it is our observation that our greatest influence has been poverty. A poor people is always intensely interested in its next meal. If you can show a Sicilian something edible that he has not already tried to eat, you will have a very surprised Sicilian—not to mention a very grateful one. We do not affect a pose that the food of other nations is beneath us. After all, we are not French.

 # Salad with Oil and Vinegar
Insalata all' Olio e Aceto

The following recipe, a simple salad dressed with oil and vinegar, calls for fresh basil. These days it's fairly easy to find fresh basil at the store, but you might, of course, grow your own. Most nurseries carry the herb, which is not only inexpensive but transplants well.

In New York, the Italian sections of the city always smelled of basil after a rain because most families grew their own in windowsill pots. I must admit that most Greek neighborhoods also smelled of basil—for the same reason. New York is a place where a blind man can wander from one ethnic neighborhood to another using only his nose to guide him.

But come, I must instruct you in the preparation of oil and vinegar salads.

You will need:

1	large head romaine lettuce	2 tsp	dried oregano
1	head escarole	1 tbsp	fresh, chopped basil leaves
5	green onions, trimmed and chopped	1 tsp	onion salt
2	zucchini, peeled and sliced	½ tsp	garlic salt
1	bell pepper, cut into strips	½ tsp	celery salt
juice of 1 lemon		black pepper to taste	
½ cup	extra virgin olive oil	4 tbsp	wine vinegar (red or white)
		salt to taste	

Preparation:

Wash and pat dry the romaine and escarole (discarding the outer leaves), and cut into bite-size chunks. Place lettuce in a large salad bowl. Combine remaining ingredients except the vinegar and salt, and mix well. You can now refrigerate the salad until ready to use.

Just before serving, add the vinegar along with the salt. Adding the vinegar too soon makes the salad taste harsh. You may already know that, but I thought a reminder would do no harm. Also, if you cannot get fresh basil, I recommend you use none at all.

Serves 6–8.

I OFTEN SUGGEST you grow your own ingredients, such as basil, since the dried variety is so inferior. I also recommend you grow your own tomatoes, particularly the plum (or pear) kind. They are best for sauces and salads. At the same time, I would be remiss if I did not warn you that these tomato plants are not at all cooperative, and unless forced to do otherwise, will not produce anything except stem and leaves.

I have a theory about tomato plants. Even the best of them are not to be trusted. Anyone who has tried to grow them has noticed the problems: first, getting them to keep the little yellow flowers long enough to produce fruit; and, second, keeping the fruit long enough to do you some good.

When all is said and done, the tomato is a self-centered jerk. Its maturity level, albeit higher than the average teenager's, is still much lower than a dog's. It assumes little responsibility for the present and has absolutely no interest in posterity.

There is only one way to get the tomato to act like a self-respecting plant: you must scare it to death! Oh, I do not mean you actually murder the thing. That is unprofitable. But you can withhold water and care from it for a week or more at a time, so that it comes to believe its demise is imminent. If you can once get the plant to say, "My God, I'm going to die!" you will finally get it to grow tomatoes. Nothing less than this will work.

I realize this advice is harsh, perhaps even brutal. But I have lost all patience with permissive fools who will squander the future by their misdirected gestures of kindness. It will not work, neither with tomatoes nor teenagers, and this is my final word on the subject.

 ## *Sicilian Potato and Green Bean Salad*

Insalata di Patate e Fagiolini alla Siciliana

You will need:

2 lbs	small new potatoes	½ tsp	garlic salt
I lb	tender green beans	½ tsp	black pepper
3	green onions	4 tbsp	extra virgin olive oil,
	(4″ of white only), sliced		maybe a little more
2 tbsp	fresh, chopped basil leaves	3 tbsp	red wine vinegar
I tsp	dried oregano		juice of half a lemon
½ tsp	onion salt		salt to taste
			touch of sugar (optional)

Preparation:

Boil potatoes until they are firm but tender. Immerse them in cold water, drain, and allow to cool. Boil green beans to the same consistency, plunge into cold water, and drain. Cut potatoes into bite-size chunks. Cut beans into 1″ pieces.

Combine all ingredients except the vinegar, lemon juice, and salt. Refrigerate the rest, adding them when ready to serve. You may consider adding a little sugar if the lemon is too tart.

Serves 6–8.

 *Starving People's Potato Salad*
Insalata di Patate per i Morti di Fame

If you expect a large and ravenous group of guests, consider throwing together this dish to stave off the barbarians. *Morti di fame* is local dialect for people with an enormous appetite. It comes from the term *"morire di fame,"* which is Italian for "dying of starvation."

You will need:

5 lbs	potatoes, boiled, peeled, and irregularly sliced	2	hard-cooked eggs, sliced
½ cup	extra virgin olive oil		salt and pepper to taste
4 tbsp	white wine vinegar		handful of fresh, chopped parsley
3 tsp	sugar		paprika (for sprinkling)

Preparation:

Combine potatoes, oil, vinegar, sugar, and salt and pepper. Then sprinkle with parsley, the sliced eggs, and a bit of paprika.

That should fix them!

Feeds 1–10.

Marinated Green Olives
OLIVE VERDI MARINATE

This recipe and the one following are typically Sicilian: tasty but time-consuming. And since any Italian deli worth its salt carries these items, why bother to make them at home?

But if you do, the preparation time is 1–2 hours—plus the number of days you let the olives marinate. Obviously, they cannot qualify as "fast food." Also, you might wish to halve the recipes so that they are more manageable. These recipes are from the deli that the Old Man ran in Los Angeles for 10 years.

You will need:

4 quarts	brined green olives with pits, crushed individually with a wooden mallet (break each olive open, but do not crush pits)	I cup	cocktail onions, rinsed
8	large celery stalks, cut in large pieces	I	pint jar of sweet peppers, cut into strips
I cup	mildly pickled cauliflower, rinsed (available in Italian stores and some supermarkets)	4 tbsp	dried oregano
		2 tbsp	black pepper
		½ cup	extra virgin olive oil (a bit more if you wish)
		3–3 ½ cups	dry white wine

Preparation:

Combine all ingredients in a very large glass jar or ceramic crock with a lid. Mix well. Rotate the ingredients each day for at least three days. Do not eat the pits!

Hot Spiced Black Olives
Olive alla Siciliana

Again, the preparation takes 1–2 hours—plus the time you let the ingredients sit. Halve the recipe if you prefer.

You will need:

2 quarts	black oil-cured olives	1 tbsp	black pepper, coarsely ground
1 cup	extra virgin olive oil	2 tbsp	dried oregano
3 tbsp	crushed red pepper	1 tsp	dried tarragon

Preparation:

Combine all ingredients in a large glass jar or ceramic crock with a lid. Mix well. Let sit at least one day.

Vegetables and Stuffings

Verdure e Ripieni

TTEND! I shall share with you an interesting thing. Americans do not care for vegetables. They do not pick string beans or pea pods one at a time, or show an interest in the age of a squash or a melon. Instead, they thrust a handful of green things into a bag, splash the contents into a pot of boiling water, and, finally, poke impatiently at them with a fork so they will die more quickly. It is their fundamental restlessness that does them harm. Look how they've taken to frozen foods, even when what's inside the package tastes the same as the package itself.

Notice the success of their restaurants that sell only sandwiches. Americans, I am told, will eat anything—provided it is "sandwiched" between two pieces of bread. I might add that the sandwich must be quartered and held together by toothpicks ending in frazzled strips of colored cellophane. Also, it is required that withered bits of lettuce leak from the edges.

I only object because taking time to eat well is so enjoyable. A southerner would understand this. And not just a southern Italian. Ah, no! Even in this strange and wonderful land, the people of the south have learned to escape the affliction of bicarbonate of soda. It is useless, however, to mention midwestern folks, since their food is shipped frozen to them from other parts of the country. The north, if it boasts any kind of food at all, contents itself with boiled codfish, beans, and a thing called "hash." Hash is extracted from cans. Once free, it achieves a gray color and an odd smell that is offensive to cats.

In Italy, the same geographical distinctions apply. Now, at this point, it is conceivable that northern Italians may object. I recommend that no attention be paid to them, since they are a minority and usually persons of no particular consequence. There is even some doubt that they are truly Italian. My sainted father was fond of pointing out that "anything north of Palermo is Swiss!" I understand these strange people attain great height (greater than 5′6″), are often pale, have impossibly colored eyes, and eat corn. There was one celebrated specimen on display in Messina some years back who sported freckles.

The subject is frivolous, of course, and I am concerned only inasmuch as the problem may be a product of improper diet. In all honesty, though, it could very well be a glandular condition.

The northern language, too, is thick and garbled and said to be related to Italian. If true, what a sad commentary on the perversions that time and distance can foist upon a once noble tongue.

It occurs to me that some northerners may find this book objectionable. It would be ignoble and contemptible for them to do so, and would demonstrate their mean-spirited but innate ethnic prejudice. Still, what can one expect from a bunch of *mangiapolentas* (cornmeal eaters)? It appears I have digressed. Unhappily, it is a frequent fault but one that I am willing to share with friends. And since others do not matter, I am sure to be forgiven. In which case, let me return to talk of vegetables.

The Enterprising Artichoke

THERE IS perhaps somewhere a great artist waiting to do justice to the miracle of artichokes. Unfortunately, I am a mere mechanic. But I will say what I can, and hope that my poor best suffices.

Artichokes, like apples, discolor as you clean them, so it is a good idea to have an acid bath (mix a gallon of water with some lemon juice or vinegar) available. Also, I would not recommend using iron or steel utensils. (A stainless steel utensil can be used, but avoid carbon or rolled steel.) Not only will the artichoke discolor, but it will take on a metallic taste.

If you steam or bake your artichokes, be sure to cover them or they will dry out. If you have no pan cover, use a clean cloth. You may want to place each artichoke in a teacup or a dessert dish when baking. This way, it will not fall over into the liquid in the pan.

Some things should be avoided. Do not boil artichokes, or they will be waterlogged and tasteless. Steam them instead. And don't broil them or try to eat them raw—you'll tear out your teeth. Alternatively, you can bake them or fry them or cook them in a pie with ricotta cheese. You can even make them into puffy soufflés, marinate them for salads, fold them into omelets, or use them in antipasto.

In old Sicily, many small inns made their own wine, and much of it was not worth drinking. But the wine sellers had a trick to keep their customers happily in ignorance of just how bad the wine was. They would gather small mountain artichokes *(carciofi di montagna)*, setting out these morsels of bitterness free for their customers. Any wine, even if mostly vinegar, tasted sweet as nectar after you munched on a few of these.

Stuffed Artichokes
Carciofi Ripieni

Before you begin, set out 6 teacups or similarly shaped receptacles.

You will need:

6	medium artichokes	2	cloves garlic, finely minced
2 tbsp	lemon juice or vinegar (for water bath)	¼ lb	hard salami, finely chopped
2 cups	Seasoned Bread Crumbs (see page 59)	¼ lb	provolone or other hard cheese, finely chopped
½	medium onion, finely minced	4 tbsp	extra virgin olive oil

Preparation:

Cut off the bottom of each artichoke stem, leaving about ½″ below the base of the heart. Cut off the top of the artichoke, about a third down, and gently spread leaves apart. Remove the toughest outer leaves. Drop artichokes into a large pot of acidulated water (1 gallon of water with a squirt of lemon or vinegar), letting them float around while you prepare the stuffing.

Combine bread crumbs, onions, garlic, salami, and cheese in a large bowl, mixing thoroughly. One by one remove the artichokes from the bath. Hold an artichoke over the bowl, and stuff the filling between the leaves. When the gaps between leaves have all been filled, gently shake excess crumbs into the bowl and go on to the next artichoke. (Use any extra filling to spread over the artichokes.)

After an artichoke has been stuffed, set it into a cup half filled with water. Place the cups in a saucepan or pot with a tight lid (a covered roasting pan is best) and add about an inch of water to the pan.

Slowly dribble olive oil over the top of each artichoke. Cook with cover on over high heat until water boils. Reduce heat to a slow simmer and continue cooking, covered, for about 45 minutes. Test for doneness by pulling a leaf from an artichoke. When it pulls out easily, remove artichokes from the pan and allow them to cool before serving.

Serves 6.

Variation: Another Sicilian stuffing for artichokes uses the same ingredients but adds fresh parsley, capers, and crushed anchovies. The stuffing is then topped with lemon juice for added tartness. I recommend this version to anyone save those people who have a problem with anchovies, which, I might add, I consider a terrible affliction with probable metabolic causes.

Fried Artichokes
Carciofi Fritti

There are seemingly countless ways of combining artichokes with other foods in a frying pan. Usually onion and garlic are sautéed in olive oil, and then chopped parsley, fresh basil, and salt and pepper are added. The artichokes are washed and peeled down to the soft, light-green inner leaves and then sliced. These slices are added to the pan and lightly browned.

Sometimes the slices are first coated with flour and then fried in the pan. Some people even dip the floured slices into beaten egg before frying.

At any rate, after the slices have cooked a bit, some broth and wine are added to the pan and allowed to simmer. (The wine reduces as it cooks.)

Another variation is to add chopped tomatoes and basil to the artichokes and then toss in a handful of fresh peas.

Any mixture you fancy can be used to make a lovely frittata by adding a few eggs, some chopped bits of mozzarella, and a sprinkling of fresh parsley over which is grated some pungent Romano cheese. Bake at 400° to a golden brown.

If you prefer meat to eggs, you may fry a few pork chops or lamb chops—with minced garlic, sage, and rosemary pressed into the meat. When the chops are browned, lay them in an oven pan, pour the artichoke mixture over them, and bake at 375° (covered) for 10–15 minutes.

You know, it renews one's faith in a generous universe to consider the manifold methods of coaxing a tasty meal from this single plant. To realize that the plant is a thistle—a cousin to the cactus—stuns one into silence. A little encouragement, you know, will work miracles for any of us.

Artichokes can also be used to make a sauce for pasta, but I shall speak of that in another place.

Sauce for Artichokes
SALSA PER CARCIOFI

Lest I be accused of misleading you, this is a sauce to be used with artichokes. It is not a sauce made from the plant. I am sorry if you are disappointed. Still, it is a fine sauce and can do you no lasting harm.

You will need:

4 tbsp	extra virgin olive oil	2	bay leaves
2 tbsp	butter		juice of 1 lemon
2	cloves garlic, finely minced		salt and pepper to taste
½ tsp	oregano		

Preparation:

Prepare artichokes in much the same way as for stuffing them (see page 28). However, instead of stuffing, you will steam them on the stove top or in the oven.

First, Heat olive oil and butter in a small pan and sauté the garlic, oregano, and bay leaves. Remove pan from heat when the garlic is golden, and discard the bay leaves. Season the mixture with lemon juice and salt and pepper.

Pour the sauce over the artichokes, then either steam or bake them. The artichokes are done when you can easily pull out a leaf. This wonderful sauce will make them taste rich and tangy.

Yields ½ cup.

Note: Be very careful not to burn the garlic. When garlic burns, it becomes bitter tasting.

Asparagus Parmesan
Asparagi alla Parmigiana

Asparagus will taste better steamed than boiled. Whether served hot or cold (with a dash of lemon), there is really nothing to match the creamy luxury of its flavor. I am firmly convinced that the habit of taking off one's hat when sitting down to eat was originally a gesture of reverence to the wonders of asparagus—much like taking off one's shoes when approaching the Ten Commandments of Mount Sinai. Well, perhaps not that reverent.

You will need:

4 tbsp	melted butter	salt and pepper to taste	
4 tbsp	extra virgin olive oil	juice of half a lemon	
2 lbs	asparagus		
I cup	grated Romano cheese		

Preparation:

Preheat oven to 450°. Wash each stalk of asparagus well and snap off the bottom (tougher) part of the stalk. Steam upper tender shoots for 5 minutes, or until nearly done. Test with a fork.

Pour butter and oil into a casserole dish and lay asparagus on top. Sprinkle with cheese and salt and pepper.

Bake uncovered for about 5 minutes or until cheese melts. Serve hot, sprinkled with lemon juice.

Serves 4.

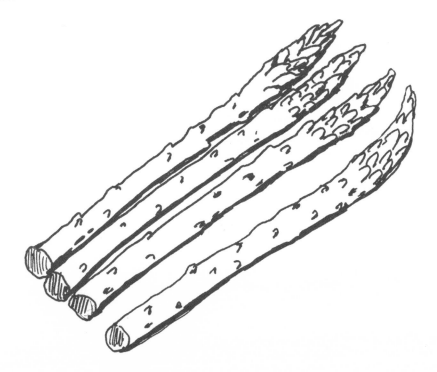

Broccoli Sautéed in Oil

Broccoli Saltati all'Olio

You will need:

2	cloves garlic, thinly sliced	salt and pepper to taste
4 tbsp	extra virgin olive oil	juice of 1 lemon (optional)
1 lb	broccoli crowns, washed and separated	

Preparation:

Steam broccoli till nearly tender, then set aside. Sauté garlic in olive oil in a small saucepan. Add steamed broccoli, along with a small amount of water, just before the garlic browns. Turn broccoli till coated with oil. Cover pan and simmer for 5 minutes. Remove and add salt and pepper.

Serves 4.

Note: Though lemon goes well with the taste of broccoli, I would not advise adding the lemon juice during the cooking. The broccoli will lose its color and turn yellow. If using, add the lemon only after the dish is served.

Variation: If you wish to expand this dish, add a can of cannellini (white kidney beans) to the pan and heat until warm.

Spinach Sautéed in Oil
Spinaci Saltati all'Olio

You will need:

3 tbsp	extra virgin olive oil	salt and pepper to taste
3	cloves garlic, minced	1 tbsp chopped nuts—pine nuts
1 lb	leaf spinach, carefully washed	are good (optional)

Preparation:

Heat olive oil in a small saucepan and sauté the garlic. Add spinach and mix gently for a few minutes, until all the leaves are coated with oil.

Cover pan loosely and simmer. Stir in salt and pepper (and nuts, if desired) after 5 minutes and cook until tender.

Serves 3–4.

Variation: Obviously, many other broadleaf vegetables, such as Swiss chard, can be treated in the same manner; so can endive and escarole, both of which are used as the base for many beautiful Sicilian soups.

Frittata

Here are two methods for creating this open-faced omelet—the first on top of the stove, and the second in the oven.

You will need:

1 lb	asparagus, precooked or steamed till tender	¼ cup	grated Romano cheese
4 tbsp	extra virgin olive oil		salt and pepper to taste
6	eggs	½ cup	mozzarella, or similar mellow cheese, cubed (Preparation 2)

Preparation 1:

Heat olive oil in a skillet and add the asparagus. Cook at low heat until warmed through. Beat eggs and cheese together and pour over asparagus.

Cook slowly, occasionally lifting the edges of the frittata and tilting the pan to allow the egg to run under, until nearly set.

Place a platter over the pan, turn upside-down, and then slide the frittata back onto the pan to brown the bottom side. Add salt and pepper before serving.

Preparation 2:

This method uses the same ingredients as above, but you add mozzarella or any other good-tasting mellow cheese.

Preheat oven to 350°. Heat olive oil in a cast iron frying pan or other ovenproof skillet, warm the asparagus in the oil, and then add the beaten eggs and Romano cheese.

Sprinkle the mozzarella over the top. Allow the bottom of the frittata to brown. Now place the entire skillet into the oven.

Bake the frittata slowly, allowing the cheese to melt and bubble. Remove from oven before adding salt and pepper.

Fried Cauliflower
Cavolfiore Fritto

You will need:

I	head cauliflower	2	eggs, well beaten
I cup	all-purpose flour	½ cup	warm water
I tbsp	corn starch	I ½ tsp	baking powder
2 tbsp	extra virgin olive oil	½ tsp	salt
		vegetable oil (approximately 4 cups)	

Preparation:

Lower cauliflower into a pot of salted, boiling water. Return water to a boil, then remove and drain the cauliflower. Separate into florets and set them aside.

Combine all other ingredients except the vegetable oil into a large bowl and beat vigorously until mixture is without lumps.

Heat vegetable oil to 375° in a deep pan or fryer. Dip each floret into the batter, then drop it into the hot oil. Do not overcrowd.

Fry for 4–5 minutes until golden brown, turning pieces so they cook evenly. Serve hot.

Serves 5–6.

CAULIFLOWER IS A much-hated vegetable in this country, yet it need not be so. It is usually boiled and accompanied by small groans. A non-Italian guest once watched with interest the respect the Old Man paid this detested food. Her curiosity broke down her ancient reservations, and she tried a piece. The result was near-disbelief in the lively flavor. The Old Man flatly pointed out (indifferent to the insult he offered the poor girl's family), "If it had been prepared correctly, you would have always liked it!" So much for polite chatter. He remained unrepentant all his life.

You know, I have a theory about vegetables. I also have a theory about tools. I advise you to buy either the best or the cheapest. Trying to compromise with something that claims to be a little bit good and a little bit cheap will bring you to calamity. But the best you will take good care of; and the cheapest can be used once and then thrown away.

But this is not my theory about vegetables. With vegetables, I suggest you grow your own. I do not mean you should cultivate a farm, for this would leave you little time to enjoy anything else. But you can grow that which you always use, such as plum tomatoes, peppers, zucchini, and perhaps some eggplant. And don't forget about sweet basil.

The rest must be bought in a store, and you must make the best of this situation. You will have noticed how Italians spend a good deal of time searching among the produce, always seeking perfection. Some have been known to stand at attention and salute a particularly fine specimen. I know of a musically inclined young man who would sing an aria from *Turandot* at the sight of a ripe melon, but this demonstration of exuberance I feel to be misplaced. Artichokes, perhaps … even an eggplant. But a melon?

My point, by the way, is that Italians have the extraordinary idea that fresh produce used immediately is half the battle. To date, no one has yet proven them wrong.

Fried Squash Blossoms
Fritto di Fiori di Zucca

If you grow squash of any kind, you are lucky in that you will be provided with the big, puffy orange flowers that precede the fruit. They are quite wonderful when stuffed and fried. You will, of course, have to leave enough of them on the vine to guarantee getting the squash as well—but that's no great problem.

You will need:

12	unopened squash blossoms	salt and pepper to taste
½ cup	mozzarella cheese, diced	all-purpose flour (for dredging)
½ cup	grated Romano cheese	2 eggs, well beaten
½ cup	fresh parsley, chopped	4 tbsp extra virgin olive oil

Preparation:

Gently wash each flower under running water. Pat dry and set aside. Mix cheeses and parsley together and flavor with salt and pepper.

Slit each flower along the side and push cheese filling into the flower. Dredge each flower in flour and then in beaten eggs.

Heat olive oil in large skillet and gently lower filled flowers into hot oil. Brown both sides quickly.

Serve hot. A wonderful thing!

Serves 4–6.

Fried Eggplant
MELANZANE FRITTE

You will need:

1	medium eggplant	¾ cup	Seasoned Bread Crumbs
salt			(see page 59)
½ cup	all-purpose flour	½ cup	extra virgin olive oil,
2	eggs, well beaten		perhaps more
		salt and pepper to taste	

Preparation:

Peel eggplant and cut into ½″ slices. Salt the slices and place them in a colander with a weight on top. Let stand at least an hour. Rinse off salt, and pat slices dry.

Flour each slice and then individually dip first in eggs and then in bread crumbs. Bring olive oil to medium heat in a frying pan, then fry both sides to golden brown. Probe a slice with a fork to test for doneness.

Drain fried slices on paper towels and sprinkle with salt and pepper to taste.

Serves 3–4.

Note: When flash fried, eggplant can soak up too much oil and become saturated and heavy. This usually, but not always, happens if the oil is not sufficiently hot. One way to control the problem is to use just enough oil to cover the bottom of the pan; then, keep turning the slices so they don't burn. Another method is to brush on a single coating of oil and then grill the slices. Be imaginative, and all will be well.

Eggplant Parmesan
Melanzane alla Parmigiana

You'd be correct to wonder whether this is a typically Sicilian dish. But I am partial to it, and think you will be too.

You will need:

2	medium eggplants	5–6	fresh basil leaves
salt		salt and pepper to taste	
½ cup	extra virgin olive oil, perhaps more	1 tsp	sugar (optional)
		4 tbsp	sweet vermouth
3	cloves garlic, thinly sliced	¼ lb	shredded mozzarella cheese
1 can	(28 oz) plum tomatoes, crushed	¼ cup	grated Romano cheese
1 tsp	oregano		

Preparation:

Peel eggplants, then slice into ½″-thick pieces. Salt the slices and place them in a colander with a weight on top. Let stand at least an hour. Rinse and pat dry each slice.

Flash fry each slice in olive oil at high heat. (If the temperature is too low, the eggplant will absorb oil and become soggy.) Turn slices once; when both sides are golden, set them aside, keeping them warm.

Sauté garlic in the same skillet, using additional oil as necessary. Before the garlic turns brown, pour in the tomatoes, breaking them with a fork. Simmer for 10 minutes. Add oregano, basil, and salt and pepper. If desired, add sugar for a sweeter taste. Raise heat to a fast bubble and pour in the vermouth, allowing it to bubble a few minutes before removing pan from heat.

Preheat oven to 375°.

Use an ovenproof pan sufficiently deep for the eggplant and sauce (leaving room on top to prevent splashing). Spoon a bit of sauce on the bottom, then arrange the first layer of eggplant. Keep slices as close together as possible without piggy-backing. Sprinkle shredded mozzarella over the eggplant layer, then spoon more sauce on top. Add the grated Romano. Continue layering in this fashion until you have used up all the ingredients.

Bake covered for at least 30 minutes, or until you can see the sauce bubbling. Allow to sit for 10 minutes before serving.

Serves 6.

Stuffed Eggplant
Melanzane Ripiene

In this recipe you cook the whole eggplant in boiling water for about 10 minutes, then drain and cool. The eggplant is then cut in half and the pulp removed and set aside. This is only one way to go about stuffing eggplants. There are several other techniques. You could fit the halves together and tie with string so that they bake whole. (This would require more cooking time.) Another method—best for small eggplants—is to cut wedges from the whole eggplant and stuff garlic, parsley, and hard cheese into each wedge before frying in a skillet.

However, let us examine the method we are used to.

You will need:

4 tbsp	extra virgin olive oil	I tsp	oregano
2	medium eggplants	¼ tsp	nutmeg
2	cloves garlic, minced	salt and pepper to taste	
½	onion, minced	I cup	grated Romano cheese
½ lb	ground beef	I	egg, lightly beaten

Preparation:

Prepare the scooped-out eggplant halves and the pulp, as described above.

Preheat oven to 375°, and oil a large baking pan.

Heat olive oil in a large skillet and sauté the garlic and onion. Add the ground beef, and mix in oregano, nutmeg, and salt and pepper. Brown the beef, uncovered, and then transfer it to a large bowl.

Chop up the pulp and add it to the meat. Mix in the cheese and egg. Fill eggplant halves with the mixture and place them in the pan, filling side up.

Bake for 15–20 minutes. Test with fork for doneness. Serve each half as a single portion.

Serves 4.

 ## Stuffed Mushrooms with Beef Gravy
FUNGHI RIPIENI CON SALSO DI MANZO

You will need:

For the beef gravy

1 tbsp	butter
½	onion, minced
1 tbsp	all-purpose flour
1 cup	Beef Broth (see page 66)

salt and pepper to taste

For the mushrooms

12	large mushrooms
3	slices bacon
2 tbsp	extra virgin olive oil
1	onion, minced
3	cloves garlic, minced
	pepper to taste
½ cup	Seasoned Bread Crumbs (see page 59)
⅛ tsp	ground cloves

Preparation:

Make the beef gravy first. Melt butter in a saucepan and sauté the minced onion until translucent. Add flour, stirring until it browns. Add beef broth and whisk until smooth. Season with salt and pepper, removing from heat when thickened.

Wash mushrooms and remove stems. Chop stems finely and set aside. Fry bacon until crisp, then remove and crush into bits. Add oil, onion, garlic, and a bit of pepper. Sauté until onions are translucent. Remove and cool, then mix with the bacon bits.

Combine bread crumbs and ground cloves in a mixing bowl, then add the bacon and onion mixture. Blend in a little water, a spoonful at a time, to make a smooth paste. Top each mushroom cap with paste to form a dome.

Preheat oven to 375°. Arrange a layer of mushrooms in a shallow pan, spooning the gravy on top. Cover the pan with foil and bake for 20 minutes. Remove foil and place the pan under broiler for 5 minutes, or until filling has browned.

Serves 4.

The Ubiquitous Anchovy

EVENTUALLY, YOU are going to notice that many Sicilian recipes begin with a can of anchovies. Possibly you may object to the blind pursuit of this salty little rascal, wondering why the natives are so devoted to its use. The answer is loyalty—loyalty to the memory of a dusty splendor. Hats off, please. I speak of the Roman Empire.

Garum, a sauce used to season nearly every Roman dish, was the Roman equivalent of table salt. For centuries, *garum* was to Rome what soy is to Asia and chili is to Mexico. *Garum* was made by fermenting salted fish (usually tuna) in clay jars for several months. The resulting clear, golden liquid tasted nutty rather than fishy. Though both the empire and *garum* are gone, Sicily never gave up its fondness for the taste. It is the salted anchovy that, fifteen hundred years later, still salutes that ancient glory.

Interestingly, a close relative of *garum* is still made by the Inuit of the Arctic (though it is not salted) and by natives of Southeast Asia. In Thailand it is called *nam pla;* in Vietnam, *nuoc mam;* and in Cambodia, *tuk trey.*

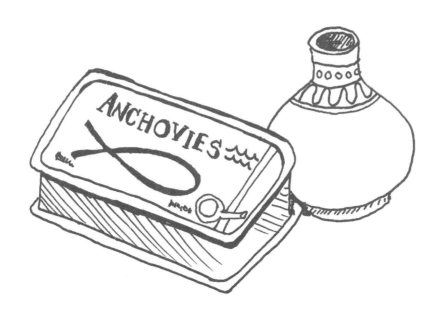

Anchovy-Stuffed Mushrooms
Funghi Ripieni con Acciughe

Here is another recipe for stuffing mushrooms. This one contains anchovies, which apparently bother some people.

You will need:

12	large mushrooms		1 tbsp	fresh parsley, minced
4 tbsp	extra virgin olive oil, plus additional for greasing		4	anchovy fillets, mashed
1	clove garlic, minced		¼ tbsp	oregano
1	onion, minced		½ tsp	salt
½ cup	Seasoned Bread Crumbs (see page 59)			

Preparation:

Wash mushrooms and separate the caps from the stems. Mince the stems and set them aside. Grease the bottom of a casserole with olive oil and set aside.

Heat olive oil in a skillet and add garlic and onion. Sauté about 5 minutes, until onions are translucent. Add the chopped stems. Stir occasionally, simmering another 3–5 minutes. Remove pan from the stove.

Preheat oven to 400°. Mix bread crumbs, parsley, anchovies, oregano, and salt and blend with the warm onion mixture until you have a moist paste. Fill the caps. Bake for 10 minutes, and serve hot.

Serves 4.

Fried Cardoon
Carduna Fritto

In the fall of each year, this item appears in stores as "cardoon" or "cardon" or even "cardune." But no matter how it's spelled, it always looks like a giant, primitive head of celery. Most people find it baffling and avoid looking at it. If you are prepared to be astonished, I shall explain the use of the thing.

You will need:

1	head cardoon	2 cups	Seasoned Bread Crumbs
4 tbsp	milk		(see page 59)
2	eggs, well beaten	½ cup	extra virgin olive oil
			salt and pepper to taste

Preparation:

Peel off the cardoon's broad outer stalks and thinner inner stalks. (You will be using all the stalks, but not the final, inner heart.) Wash each stalk and cut into sections 5–6″ long. With a paring knife, peel and discard the tough, fibrous ribbing that backs each piece.

In a large saucepan with boiling salted water, drop pieces one at a time and cook until tender. Do not overcrowd. You will find that the inner pieces take only a few minutes, but the larger outer stalks take as long as 10–15 minutes before becoming tender. Drain and dry.

Beat milk into the eggs, and then dip each stalk into the mixture. Dredge in bread crumbs. Heat olive oil in a skillet and brown the cardoon stalks on both sides at medium heat. Salt and pepper to taste. Cool on paper towels. Serve hot or cold.

Serves 6.

Note: Cardoon, like artichokes or apples, will discolor—so it's a good idea to have acidulated water (water and a squirt of vinegar or lemon) ready as you cut the stalks into pieces.

Stuffed Onions
Cipolle Imbottite

You will need:

6	large whole onions, peeled	2 cups	Seasoned Bread Crumbs
1 cup	plain bread crumbs (for topping)		(see page 59)
4 tbsp	extra virgin olive oil		salt and pepper to taste
¼ lb	ground beef	1	egg, well beaten
2 tbsp	chopped, fresh parsley		

Preparation:

Cut off the root end of each onion along with ½″ from the top. Simmer onions in salted water for about 10–15 minutes, until they are nearly tender. Drain and cool.

Heat plain bread crumbs in a skillet, then dribble in about 2 tablespoons of the olive oil. Stir and brown the crumbs, then set them aside.

Heat remaining olive oil in a skillet. Use a fork and gently scoop out the center of each parboiled onion. Chop up centers and add them to the heated oil. Add beef and stir until browned. Transfer the mixture to a bowl and blend in parsley (reserve half a tablespoon for topping) and Seasoned Bread Crumbs. Add salt and pepper, then stir in the egg to form a moist filling.

Preheat oven to 350°. Fill the onions with the mixture and place them in a casserole dish. Cover with the reserved plain bread crumbs and then sprinkle the remaining chopped parsley on top. Bake for 45 minutes.

Serves 6.

Rice and Beef Stuffed Bell Peppers

Peperoni Ripieni di Riso e Manzo

Peppers are lovely things, and it is a shame that their outer skin is as near to being indigestible as a food can get and still retain its honor. I mention this because I intend to advise you on how to remove the skin. Be alert.

You will need:

6	medium bell peppers	½ cup	Beef Broth
4 cups	Beef and Rice Stuffing		(see page 66)
	(see page 54)		

Preparation:

Prepare the beef and rice stuffing and have the beef broth ready. Preheat oven to 375°.

If your stomach can handle unskinned peppers, simply wash them and slice off the tops. Clean out the seeds, fill the peppers with the stuffing, and then replace the tops with toothpicks to hold them in place. Set the peppers upright in a casserole dish and pour in the broth. Bake covered for an hour or so. This is the simple way.

Your other choice is to sear the peppers whole under the broiler. Turn occasionally, making sure all the sides of the peppers have charred. Allow the peppers to cool, and then attack them with a paring knife. You will find the skin—as thin as a sheet of plastic—will peel off easily enough. Ah, but your troubles are just beginning.

You will also find the pepper to be quite limp. You will have to be as careful as a brain surgeon to cut around the top and remove the seeds without splitting or tearing the flesh. Now you are faced with filling the thing, which is similar to trying to stuff a live eel into a small paper bag. Of such things are heroes made, and if you persevere and succeed, you deserve a medal—or at least honorable mention. (On the other hand, bicarbonate of soda does not really taste so bad.)

The meal is worth it. If you do get that far, you need only set the stuffed peppers in a casserole dish and bake in the broth, though you can cut the baking time down to about 20–25 minutes.

Serves 6.

Roast Peppers
Peperoni Arrosto

You will need:

2 lbs	sweet red peppers, peeled and seeded and cut into strips (see recipe on opposite page)	4 tbsp	extra virgin olive oil
		1 tsp	oregano
			salt and pepper to taste

Preparation:

Preheat oven to 375°. Arrange the pepper strips in a casserole dish and then sprinkle on the olive oil, oregano, and salt and pepper. Bake uncovered for 10 minutes or so.

Serves 4.

Fried Peppers
PEPERONI FRITTI

You will need:

4 tbsp	extra virgin olive oil	1 tsp	oregano
1	small onion, sliced		salt and pepper to taste
1	clove garlic, thinly sliced	2 or 3	eggs (optional)
4	medium bell peppers, cut into strips		

Preparation:

Heat olive oil in a skillet and sauté the garlic and onion. Add the peppers when onions are translucent. Stir gently, adding the oregano and the salt and pepper. Make sure the oil coats all the pepper strips.

Cover the pan loosely and cook over medium heat, stirring occasionally. Sauté the peppers for about 15 minutes, or until they are tender.

Serves 4.

Variation: This recipe and the next one can be expanded with a few fried eggs. Add the eggs just before you remove the pan from the heat, and make sure they don't overcook. Both dishes taste fine all alone or with the eggs. Peppers are one of God's better ideas.

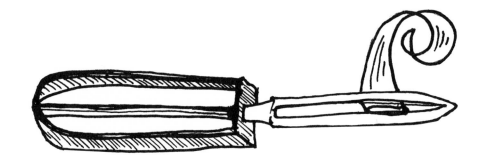

Fried Peppers and Potatoes
Peperoni e Patate Fritte

You will need:

4 tbsp	extra virgin olive oil	4	bell peppers, cut into strips
2	cloves garlic, thinly sliced		
1	medium onion, diced	1 tsp	oregano
4	medium potatoes, peeled and cubed		salt and pepper to taste
		2 or 3	eggs (optional)

Preparation:

Heat olive oil in a large skillet and sauté the garlic and onion. Add potatoes when onions are translucent. Stir until all the potatoes are coated in oil. Simmer for 10–15 minutes, stirring to prevent the potatoes from sticking. Add the peppers and stir again, adding oregano and salt and pepper as you stir.

Cook over medium heat for 15–20 minutes, stirring occasionally. Test the potatoes with a fork and, when they are tender, remove from heat. Let sit 5 minutes before serving.

Serves 4–6.

Lyonnaise Potatoes, Sicilian Style
PATATE LIONESI ALLA SICILIANA

You will need:

4 tbsp	extra virgin olive oil		I tbsp	oregano
I	onion, sliced		I tsp	thyme
2 lbs	potatoes, peeled and cut bite-size		salt and pepper to taste	
			I cup	Chicken Broth, or perhaps more (see page 66)

Preparation:

Use a large skillet with a tight-fitting lid. Heat olive oil and sauté the onion for 5 minutes. Add the potatoes and stir, coating them with oil. Sprinkle in the oregano and thyme. Add a few tablespoons of broth. Cover and cook at low heat for 10 minutes, stirring occasionally so the potatoes do not stick.

Add salt and pepper after 10 minutes, then add a bit more broth, stir, and cover again. Continue to add small amounts of broth, stirring constantly to keep the mixture moist.

After another 10–15 minutes, test the potatoes with a fork. Remove when tender, and let sit for 5 minutes before serving.

Serves 6–8.

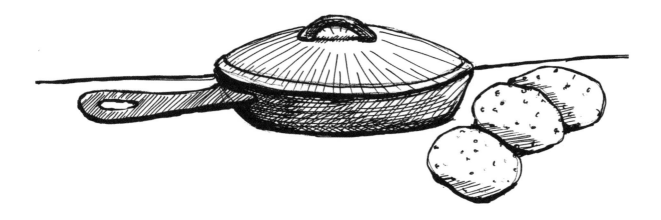

Baked Stuffed Tomatoes
Pomodori Imbottiti al Forno

You will need:

I can	(6 oz) crabmeat, picked over for fragments	½ tsp	tarragon
		½ tsp	pepper
I lb	small shrimp, shelled, deveined, and chopped	I tsp	salt
		4 tbsp	dry white wine
3	green onions (white part only), chopped	I	egg, well beaten (2nd one optional)
I	clove garlic, minced	½ cup	Seasoned Bread Crumbs (see page 59)
2	hard-cooked eggs, coarsely chopped	6	large beefsteak tomatoes
½ tsp	thyme		

Preparation:

Combine all ingredients except the tomatoes in a large mixing bowl. Blend into a moist, solid mixture that will not crumble. Add another egg if the mixture is too dry. Set aside.

Wash the tomatoes and pat dry. Slice off ½″ from the top of each (this will be the lid) and set aside. Gently core the seeded center of each tomato, being careful not to poke the knife clear through.

Pat the inside dry with a paper towel and stuff each tomato with an equal portion of the filling. Replace the tops on the tomatoes, securing with toothpicks.

Preheat oven to 350°. Transfer the stuffed tomatoes to an ovenproof pan with deep sides. Add ¼ cup water to the pan and cover tightly with foil.

Bake for 55 minutes. Remove the foil and bake an additional 10 minutes.

Serves 6.

Stuffed Zucchini
Zucchine Ripiene di Manzo e Riso

You will need:

Beef and Rice Stuffing (see page 54)

1 tbsp butter

½ onion, minced

1 tbsp all-purpose flour

2 cups Beef Broth (see page 66)

salt and pepper to taste

4 large zucchini

(should be squat, fat ones)

Preparation:

Prepare the stuffing and set aside. Then attack the sauce. Melt butter in a medium saucepan. Add onion and sauté until translucent. Add the flour gradually and blend with a whisk until smooth. Slowly add the broth, stirring vigorously, and sprinkle in salt and pepper. When the sauce starts to get thick, set it aside.

Bring a 4-quart pot of water to a boil. Drop the zucchini into the boiling water to scald for 1 minute—and no longer. Cool immediately under running water and pat dry.

Cut each zucchini in half lengthwise and scoop out the center, leaving about ¼″ of pulp. Fill each half with the stuffing, smoothing off the tops.

Preheat oven to 350°. Spoon some of the sauce on the bottom of a large casserole dish. Arrange the zucchini halves side by side, stuffing-side up. Spoon the remaining sauce over the tops.

Cover the pan tightly with foil. Bake about 50 minutes, then remove the foil and bake an additional 10 minutes.

Serves 6–8.

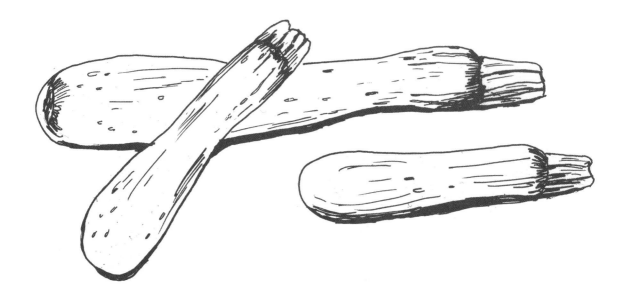

Stuffings

THOUGH SICILIANS insist upon fresh vegetables and eat many of them raw, there is no doubt they also have fallen into the habit of stuffing or filling some vegetables every chance they get. This is an old Arab trick we became addicted to—and since we found no reason to seek a cure we continue the habit, though the Arabs have long left the island.

We will stuff vegetables with meat and rice and bread crumbs and fish and cheese and even other vegetables. We generally use a lot of garlic, too, which is the source of the rich odor that clings to our foods and to ourselves.

A word on behalf of garlic. Many recipes instruct you to discard the browned garlic after it has been sautéed in hot oil. We do not do that. We view each sliver as a small soldier, who has bravely done his duty and has something more due him. Why fling him upon the ash heap? If you have the slightest sense of loyalty, you will pop each piece into your mouth with patriotic fervor. You might wish to hum a few bars of some military song.

On the other hand, for those who lack the taste for garlic, or for those who have a need to please the world (or at least remain on reasonable terms with it), fling the little criminal out for all I care. No one's feelings will be hurt.

Let us get back to our fillings. They can be used to stuff peppers or cabbage or zucchini or nearly anything else. Allow your imagination some room and see what courageous deeds can happen when you approach food seriously. Of course, I do not mean you should leave your sense of humor behind. That mistake might have you end up cooking like a German or an Englishman or some other similar curiosity.

Beef and Rice Stuffing
Ripieno di Manzo e Riso

The large green "Greek" olives are the kind my dad used.

You will need:

4 tbsp	extra virgin olive oil	1 cup	cooked rice
3	cloves garlic, minced	10	pitted green olives, chopped
1	small onion, chopped	¼ tsp	nutmeg
1 tsp	oregano	salt and pepper to taste	
1 lb	lean ground beef	1	egg, well beaten

Preparation:

Heat olive oil in a large skillet with a tight-fitting cover, then sauté the garlic, onion, and oregano. Add the beef when the onion is translucent. Stir and cover. Reduce heat and let simmer, stirring occasionally, for 15 minutes. Remove the cover and allow the juices to evaporate. Remove skillet from the heat and transfer the ingredients to a large mixing bowl.

Stir in the cooked rice, olives, nutmeg, and salt and pepper. Fold in the egg when the mixture is well blended.

Continue to mix until the filling is moist and solid. If it seems a little dry, add some water, a tablespoon at a time, until the mixture firms up.

Yields 4 cups.

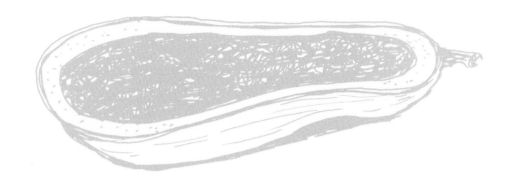

 **Beef and Bread Crumb Filling**
RIPIENO DI MANZO E PANGRATTATO

You will need:

4 tbsp	extra virgin olive oil	1 lb	lean ground beef
2 tbsp	butter	10	pitted green olives, chopped
1	small onion, chopped	1 tbsp	capers
3	cloves garlic, minced	salt to taste	
1	large green bell pepper, diced	1 cup	Seasoned Bread Crumbs
1 tsp	oregano		(see page 59)
black pepper to taste		1	egg, well beaten

Preparation:

Heat olive oil and butter in a skillet with a tight-fitting cover. Add onion, garlic, bell pepper, oregano, and black pepper. Cover pan and cook over medium heat until the diced pepper is limp, but not fully done. Add the ground beef; stir, and cover. Cook over medium heat for 15 minutes, stirring occasionally.

Add the olives, capers, and salt. Stir and simmer with the cover off until most of the juice evaporates. Remove from heat and transfer to a large mixing bowl.

Add the egg and seasoned bread crumbs, blending the mixture until it is firm but moist.

Yields 4 cups.

Shrimp and Rice Stuffing
Ripieno di Riso e Gamberi

Peppers, zucchini, and cabbage leaves are all good receptacles for this stuffing. So are crêpes, and even blintzes.

You will need:

3 tbsp	extra virgin olive oil		1 lb	small shrimp, shelled, deveined, and chopped
1 tbsp	butter		3 cups	cooked rice
½	onion, minced		1 tsp	horseradish
3	cloves garlic, minced		1 tsp	fresh ginger, grated
1 tsp	thyme		¼ cup	pitted black olives, chopped
1 tsp	tarragon		1	egg, well beaten
black pepper to taste			salt to taste	

Preparation:

Heat olive oil and butter in a large skillet. Sauté the garlic and onion, adding the thyme, tarragon, and pepper. Add shrimp when onions are translucent, stirring gently. Cover and simmer for 15 minutes. Stir frequently.

Transfer the mixture to a large mixing bowl. Add all the other ingredients, ending with the egg. Blend well and refrigerate.

Yields 5 cups.

Stuffed Rice Balls
ARANCINI

The name of this dish literally translates as "little oranges," because that's what the rice balls resemble. Should you have the good fortune to travel to Sicily, you will find *arancini* in just about every food store, deli, bar, and restaurant in every town or village or crossroads you reach. Usually they are vegetarian and use tomato sauce for color. Our recipe is a meat stuffing and uses saffron, which is older and more authentic.

You will need:

2 tbsp	salt	⅛ tsp	powdered saffron
2 cups	rice (raw), long-grain		(yes, it is very expensive)
	or other variety	I	recipe for Filling for Stuffed Rice
3 cups	plain, toasted bread crumbs		Balls (see page 58)
I tsp	salt	2	eggs, well beaten
½ tsp	celery salt	4 tbsp	milk
½ tsp	onion salt	2 cups	all-purpose flour
2 tbsp	melted butter		bread crumbs for rolling the rice balls
			(about 2 cups)
		4 cups	vegetable oil

Preparation:

Fill a 6-quart pot within 2″ of the top with water, and add 2 tablespoons of salt. Bring to a brisk boil and stir in the rice. Reduce to a low boil and cook at least 20 minutes, stirring frequently. Allow rice to overcook somewhat. Transfer the drained rice to a colander, rinse it with cold water, and set aside to drain.

Mix the toasted bread crumbs, teaspoon of salt, celery salt, and onion salt in a large bowl. Set aside.

Place the drained rice in another bowl. Add melted butter to the rice, then stir in the saffron. The rice should adhere when pressed together. Now you are ready to make the filling (recipe follows).

When the filling is ready, mix together the beaten eggs and the milk.

To make the rice balls, place 2 tablespoons of rice in the palm of your hand. Add a tablespoon of filling and fold the rice around it as you close your hand. Roll each rice ball first in the flour, then in the egg/milk mixture, and then in the bread crumbs.

Heat the oil to 375° in a deep fryer. Gently lower the rice balls into the oil, turning for a uniform golden color. Do not crowd. Serve warm, not hot—but certainly not cold.

Serves 6–8.

 **Filling for Stuffed Rice Balls**

Ripieno per Arancini

You will need:

4 tbsp	extra virgin olive oil		1 ½ lbs	lean ground beef
3	cloves garlic, minced		¼ lb	mushrooms, chopped
1	onion, finely chopped		1 tbsp	capers, chopped
1	small green bell pepper, diced		1 tsp	salt
1	rounded tsp oregano		½ tsp	nutmeg
½ tsp	black pepper		1 tbsp	dry white wine

Preparation:

Heat olive oil in a large covered skillet, then sauté the garlic, onion, bell pepper, oregano, and black pepper. Add the beef when the onion is translucent. Allow to simmer, stirring occasionally, until the meat is browned. Add mushrooms and capers and cover the pan. Simmer for 5 minutes.

Uncover and continue to stir until the juices have nearly evaporated. (Check that the beef has cooked through.) Remove from heat, transfer mixture to a mixing bowl, and allow to cool before adding salt, nutmeg, and wine.

Blend well. Now it's ready.

Yields 4 cups.

Seasoned Bread Crumbs
PANGRATTATO ALLE ERBE

Seasoned bread crumbs are used to stuff foods from artichokes to clams. They are also used as a coating for fried poultry, meat, fish, and vegetables. I have frozen crumbs in zippered freezer bags for up to a year. Having the bread crumbs available not only saves time when preparing other foods, but also inspires me to do more than fry an egg for lunch.

You will need:

1 lb	coarse bread crumbs (about 4½–5 cups)	½ tbsp	dried basil
¾ cup	grated Romano cheese	1 tsp	salt
2 tbsp	dried parsley	½ tsp	black pepper
1½ tbsp	oregano	½ tsp	garlic salt
		½ tsp	onion salt

Preparation:

Combine all ingredients until well blended. Place in air-tight jar and refrigerate.

Yields 8 cups.

Roasted Bread Crumbs
Mollica Arrostiti

Sicilians use bread crumbs as a topping for pasta, vegetables, soups, and salads. One particularly fine treatment is to roast (or brown) bread crumbs as follows. Roasted bread crumbs can be stored almost indefinitely in the refrigerator. They'll last for as long as they're kept cold and dry.

You will need:

2 cups   coarse bread crumbs

4 tbsp   extra virgin olive oil

2   cloves garlic, minced

salt and pepper to taste

Preparation:

Heat olive oil in a small skillet and stir in the garlic. Before the garlic browns add the bread crumbs, salt, and pepper. Stir until the bread crumbs are golden brown. Remove and cool.

Soups and Stews
Minestre e Stufati

 HAVE OBSERVED a thing that is neither new nor remarkable, but I shall remark upon it anyway because it is worthy of respect. It is this: the "staff of life" is not bread or pasta—it is soup! In one form or another, soup has carried our species forward when all else failed. For poor people (meaning most people throughout the centuries), soup has been the mainstay of survival. It has been our finest triumph over hunger and despair.

Who has not, at least once, been nourished from some shock or catastrophe by a bowl of warm, savory soup? Who has not been granted that extra little ounce of courage from its homey, unassuming sustenance and been able to face a world that had been put right again

On some far-off day when the human race achieves sanity and wisdom at last; when erecting statues to our most energetic and inventive murderers has lost its flavor; when not just living but living well becomes the obtainable goal of all cultures—on that day we will make a monument to this great friend of humanity. I perceive it towering above all churches and cathedrals, ministries and marketplaces—a great block of white marble in the shape of an enormous tureen of soup, perched, like the fabled cornucopia, on the gnarled shoulders of a benevolently smiling Sicilian. Thus, the full and final recognition of this ancient ally, who, when all else failed, lent to us the dignity of a full belly.

Lest I be accused of parochialism, I am willing to perceive the figure supporting this prize to be of some nationality other than Sicilian. It was merely a suggestion. I stand with complete impartiality. Make the figure a Calabrese for all I care. Perhaps even a Neapolitan, though this would be extreme.

A Good Broth

BROTH IS GOOD in any language or on any stomach. It is cheap, easy to make, and serves a variety of good uses. It can be refrigerated or even frozen. I have used it in place of water, whether we were basting "oven goods" or making sauces, gravies, or soups. I have even used broth in place of water when making bread.

As a boy, when I was sick or needed something soothing in the stomach, my mother would set a small pot of broth to boil and then throw in a handful of pastina, which are small chips of pasta often sold as "baby food." As soon as the pasta cooked, the pot was whipped off the stove and a raw egg dropped in and beaten. With a little salt and grated cheese added to the pot, one had a meal fit for a child or an old man, or perhaps one who had too well indulged in wine the night before.

The secret of its redemptive powers is, of course, the magical and mysterious thing about broth—a thing known also to Jewish mothers, who were possibly informed of it by visiting Romans some years back. I suggest this only as idle speculation since, as you may have guessed, I have no great interest in history.

Ah, well, enough. Let us be serious and talk of food.

Beef Broth
Brodo di Manzo

You will need:

3 lbs	beef neck bones		1	medium onion, finely chopped
1 cup	diced carrots			salt and pepper to taste
1 cup	celery, finely chopped			

Preparation:

Combine all ingredients with 3 quarts water in a 6-quart pot and cook 1½ hours or until liquid is reduced to 2 quarts. Cool and strain through a fine sieve.

Serves 6–8.

Chicken Broth
Brodo di Pollo

Use 3–4 lbs of chicken backs, and follow the preparation (using the same vegetables and seasonings) in the Beef Broth recipe.

Chicken Backs

REGARDING CHICKEN backs … a canny marketer will see at once that there is great promise here. They are cheaper even than the bird's feathers, and invite the imagination to consider further use for them. Many Americans, having never made broth, would resign the carcass to the garbage, and there the matter would end. Amazing! Among the wonders of this land is not only what its people are willing to ingest, but also what they cheerfully throw away.

You might, at least, feed the meat of the backs to your dog. Mind you, I have nothing against your dog and introduce him only to emphasize a point: why should he eat better than you?

But again I become obscure. Come, let us forget about your dog. After all, what could he know? Anyone who can acquire the mange or be unable to free himself from the mildest infestation of body fleas is hardly an authority on gourmet food. Also, dogs do not live long. Possibly this is the result of an improper diet. I do not know this for a fact, but suggest it to demonstrate my flair for scientific speculation.

If, at this time, you find yourself with an educated smirk on your face, I invite you to close this book at once. We are cooks, not literary dilettantes, and I write only for people with great stomachs and good hearts!

Returning to chicken backs. It seems reasonable that the meat can be extracted and joined with macaroni to make an interesting salad or a filling, such as for cannelloni. The skin can be rendered down and ground with fried onion to make a filling for biscuits. The rendered chicken fat, too, may be used in a variety of ways, particularly if one has a taste for Jewish cooking—but this goes beyond the scope of this book.*

---

*The Old Man loved food and would try anything from kosher to Cantonese. He did not affect a disdain for other people's cuisine since, as he was fond of saying, he was not French, and his other habits were good.

Fish Broth

BRODO DI PESCE

You will need:

2 lbs	fish heads		I	bay leaf
I cup	celery tops, finely chopped		I	pinch thyme
I	medium onion, finely chopped		I cup	dry white wine
2–3	sprigs parsley		3 cups	water
			salt and pepper to taste	

Preparation:

Bring all ingredients to a boil in a large pot. Lower the heat and simmer for 20 minutes. Strain the stock into a serving bowl or tureen.

Serves 6–8.

Beef Soup with Tiny Meatballs

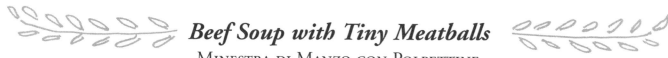

MINESTRA DI MANZO CON POLPETTINE

You will need:

I lb	lean ground beef		I	egg, well beaten
¼ cup	Seasoned Bread Crumbs		2	quarts Beef Broth
	(see page 59)			(see page 66)
½	small onion, minced		¼ lb	vermicelli, broken
3	cloves garlic, minced			into small pieces
salt and pepper to taste			¼ cup	grated Romano cheese

Preparation:

Combine the first 6 ingredients in a large mixing bowl. Mix thoroughly to form a firm but moist consistency. Using a ½-teaspoon measure, scoop up a portion into your palm and form a tiny meatball, repeating until mixture is used up. Set meatballs aside.

Bring beef broth to a boil in a 4-quart saucepan and add vermicelli. Cook for 3 minutes, stirring several times. Add meatballs. Cook for 8–10 minutes, or until vermicelli is done to your taste.

Serve in individual bowls and sprinkle with grated cheese.

Serves 6–8.

 ## Chicken Soup with Tiny Chicken Morsels
MINESTRA DI POLLO CON POLPETTINE

You will need:

2 quarts	Chicken Broth, plus 2 tbsp to moisten the mixture (see page 66)	2 tsp	finely chopped fresh parsley
		1 tsp	oregano
		½	onion, minced
1 lb	ground chicken meat	3	cloves garlic, minced
¼ cup	plain bread crumbs	1	egg, well beaten
¼ lb	vermicelli, broken into small pieces	¼ cup	grated Romano cheese
		salt and pepper to taste	

Preparation:

Set aside the 2 quarts of chicken broth and the vermicelli.

Combine in a mixing bowl all the remaining ingredients except the cheese. Mix thoroughly to form a firm but moist consistency.

Using a ½-teaspoon measure, scoop up a portion into your palm and form a tiny meatball, repeating until the mixture is used up. Set meatballs aside.

Bring broth to a boil in a 4-quart saucepan and add vermicelli. Cook for 3 minutes, stirring several times. Add meatballs. Cook for 8–10 minutes, or until vermicelli is done to your taste.

Serve in individual bowls and sprinkle with grated cheese.

Serves 6–8.

Clam Soup
Zuppe di Vongole

This recipe has you immerse the clams for 10 hours or overnight.

You will need:

24	cherrystone clams (immerse in cold water for 10 hours or overnight)	3 lbs	plum tomatoes, peeled and chopped
⅓ cup	extra virgin olive oil	½ cup	dry white wine
2	cloves garlic, chopped		salt and pepper to taste
			handful of fresh parsley, chopped
			fresh lemon juice (optional)

Preparation:

Heat olive oil in a 6-quart pot and sauté garlic for 1 minute before adding the chopped tomatoes. Bring to a boil and add the wine. Reduce heat and simmer for 15 minutes. Add salt and pepper. (This mix is called *soffritto*, a vegetable base for sauces and soups.) Transfer *soffritto* to a bowl; set to one side.

Scrub the clams and place into the same pot with 1 cup of boiling water. Cover tightly, reduce the heat, and steam the clams until they open, about 5 minutes. (Discard any clams that remain closed.) Strain the juice into the *soffritto*.

Place the open clams into soup bowls. Return *soffritto* and clam juice to the pot to simmer for 2 minutes, then pour the liquid over the clams. Sprinkle fresh parsley and lemon juice over the top.

Serves 4–6.

Note: Clams should never be cooked more than a few minutes or they will become like small bits of gritty rubber, undeserving of either you or your guests.

Clam Chowder
Minestrone alle Vongole

This recipe calls for 2 cups of chopped clams. Canned clams work perfectly fine, but if using fresh, be sure to discard any that don't open.

You will need:

2 cups	chopped clams (reserve the juice)	1½ cups	diced potatoes
4 tbsp	extra virgin olive oil	1 quart	Chicken Broth (see page 66)
1	medium onion, coarsely chopped	1 can	(28 oz) crushed plum tomatoes
1 tbsp	thyme		
1 tsp	oregano	1 tsp	sugar
salt and pepper to taste		4 tbsp	dry white wine
1 cup	diced celery	½ cup	fresh parsley, chopped
1 cup	diced carrots		grated Romano cheese

Preparation:

Heat olive oil in a 6-quart pot with a tight-fitting cover, then sauté the onion for 5 minutes at medium heat. Add the thyme, oregano, and salt and pepper. Stir in the celery and carrots. Cook covered for 15 minutes. Add the potatoes and cook another 10 minutes, stirring occasionally to avoid sticking. If mixture starts to stick, add ½ cup of the broth.

Add broth and tomatoes. Bring to a boil and add the sugar and wine. Reduce heat to simmer, and cook another 15 minutes or until potatoes are tender.

Add the clam juice and allow mixture to warm. Adjust for seasonings.

Add the clams, bringing the chowder to a slow boil. Remove from heat immediately. Cover the pot, then set aside for about 5 minutes before serving. Sprinkle grated cheese and fresh parsley over individual servings.

Serves 6–8.

Mussel Soup
ZUPPE DI AFFOGATI

You will need:

½ cup   extra virgin olive oil

1   clove garlic, thinly sliced

1   medium onion, diced

½ cup   celery, chopped

salt and pepper to taste

½ cup   dry white wine

handful fresh, chopped basil leaves

3   medium tomatoes, chopped

4   dozen mussels

grated lemon peel (for garnish)

Preparation:

Heat olive oil and sauté the garlic for 1 minute. Add the onion, celery, and salt and pepper. Cook for 5 minutes at medium heat, and then add the wine. Bring to a brisk boil and allow the wine to reduce by half. Add basil and tomatoes and simmer, covered, for a further 20 minutes.

Scrub the mussels with a stiff brush and remove the beards.

Drop the mussels into the wine and vegetable mixture. Cover and simmer, shaking the pot every now and then until the mussels have opened. (Discard any unopened mussels.)

Remove from heat. Spoon the mussels into serving bowls and cover with the broth. Sprinkle grated lemon peel on top.

Serves 4–6.

Note: To feel really Italian, fry slices of seeded Italian bread in olive oil, place the bread in the bowls, and pour the soup on top.

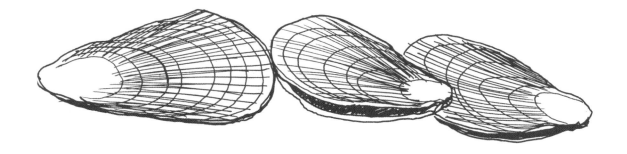

Escarole Soup
ZUPPE DI SCAROLA

You will need:

1	head escarole	salt and pepper to taste
4 tbsp	extra virgin olive oil	pinch of nutmeg
1 tbsp	butter	4 cups Chicken Broth
2	cloves garlic, minced	(see page 66)
1	small onion, finely diced	½ cup shell or elbow macaroni
¼ tsp	thyme	grated Romano cheese
¼ tsp	oregano	

Preparation:

Wash and drain the escarole, then cut it into strips after discarding the coarse outer leaves.

Heat olive oil and butter in a 6-quart pot, then sauté the garlic and onion until the onion turns translucent. Add thyme, oregano, and salt and pepper.

Mix the escarole in with the garlic and onion. Simmer 5 minutes and dust with nutmeg. Add broth, stir, and bring to a boil. Add macaroni and stir. (If you wish a thinner soup, parboil, rinse, and drain the macaroni before adding it to the broth.)

Cook until the macaroni is done, about 10–15 minutes. Serve with grated cheese sprinkled on individual servings.

Serves 4.

Variation: Feel free to replace the escarole with endive or any other sharp or bitter-leafed green vegetable.

Lentil Soup
ZUPPE DI LENTICCHIE

You will need:

4 tbsp	extra virgin olive oil	I lb	lentils, washed and screened for stones
3	cloves garlic, sliced	4 tbsp	dry white wine
¼ lb	diced ham or sliced bacon	I quart	Chicken or Beef Broth (see page 66)
I cup	chopped green onions		salt and pepper to taste
I cup	celery, diced		grated Romano cheese
I cup	carrots, diced		
I tbsp	dried basil		
I tbsp	oregano		

Preparation:

Heat olive oil in a large saucepan, then sauté the garlic and the diced ham or bacon. Stir occasionally for 5 minutes and then add the onions, celery, and carrots. Stir in the basil and oregano and simmer 10 minutes longer, continuing to stir so that the vegetables and meat don't stick.

Add the lentils to the pot and stir in the wine. Bring to a boil, then wait for the wine to boil off. Add the broth. Cook over moderate heat for about an hour, or until the lentils are tender. Season with salt and pepper.

Serve with grated cheese.

Serves 4–6.

Minestrone

EVERY REGION has its own variation of this popular soup. The word literally means "to hand out," which refers to the thick soup that monks prepared over a fire to hand out to travelers. The original soup had a bean base, usually with a meat or chicken stock in which vegetables—which varied according to the season—were cooked. The following two minestrone recipes use beans as a base. The first is made with dried beans and the second, for those in a hurry, uses canned beans.

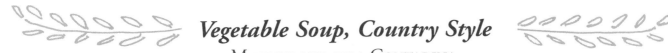 

Vegetable Soup, Country Style
Minestrone alla Contadina

You will need:

1 lb	dried pink or pinto beans, soaked overnight	5	stalks celery, diced
4 quarts	Chicken or Beef Broth (see page 66)	1 lb	carrots, diced
		2 tbsp	oregano
extra broth or wine (for a thinner soup)		1 tbsp	dried basil
½ lb	salt pork or 1 ham bone	salt and pepper to taste	
½ cup	extra virgin olive oil	1 lb	potatoes, diced
4	cloves garlic, thinly sliced	1 can	butter beans or package frozen baby lima beans
1	large onion, chopped	½ lb	spaghettini, broken
1	small head cabbage, shredded	grated Romano cheese	

Preparation:

You can either first soak the dried beans overnight or place them in a large pot with the broth. In either case, bring them to a hard boil for 5 minutes before setting them aside, covered, for an hour.

Return the pot to the burner, adding the salt pork or ham bone. Bring to a boil, then lower the heat and simmer, covered, for 1½–2 hours. The beans should be tender. Discard the bone, and with a slotted spoon strain out half the beans. Mash the strained-out beans into a purée, using some of the stock. Return the purée to the pot. Stir together the purée, stock, and whole beans and set the pot aside.

Heat olive oil in a large saucepan, and sauté the garlic and onion for 5 minutes. Add the shredded cabbage and simmer for 5 minutes. Add the celery and carrots. Sprinkle in the herbs and salt and pepper, mix well, and simmer 10 minutes before adding the potatoes. Simmer another 5 minutes, add the reserved bean mixture and stock, bring to a boil, and then add the canned or frozen beans. Cover and simmer for 30 minutes, stirring occasionally and testing the carrots and potatoes until they seem half-cooked.

Drop in the broken spaghettini and stir. The pasta will absorb some of the broth as it cooks and will help to create a thick soup that's nearly a stew. Add additional broth or dry white wine if you want a thinner soup. Remove from heat when the pasta is done. Spoon the stew into bowls. Sprinkle with grated cheese.

Serves 6–8.

Quick Minestrone
MINESTRONE SBRIGATIVO

You will need:

½ cup	extra virgin olive oil		I	small head cabbage, shredded
3	cloves garlic, thinly sliced		I can	(28 oz) peeled plum tomatoes
I	large onion, coarsely chopped		I can	(15 oz) red kidney beans, drained
I lb	carrots, diced			
5	stalks celery, diced		I can	(15 oz) white kidney beans (cannellini), drained
2 tbsp	oregano			
I tbsp	dried basil		I can	(15 oz) chick peas (garbanzo beans), drained
salt and pepper to taste				
4 quarts	Beef or Chicken Broth (see page 66)		I can	(15 oz) baby lima beans
			I cup	small shell macaroni
I lb	potatoes, diced		grated Romano cheese	

Preparation:

Heat olive oil in a large pot, then sauté the garlic and onion for 5 minutes. Add the carrots, celery, oregano, basil, and salt and pepper, and simmer an additional 15 minutes. Stir to prevent sticking. Add the broth, potatoes, and cabbage. Bring to a boil, then reduce heat and cook for 15 minutes.

Crush the tomatoes in a bowl, then add them to the pot, along with the drained kidney beans (both varieties), chick peas, and baby limas. Add additional salt and pepper to taste, and return the mixture to a slow boil.

Add the macaroni and cook 15 minutes or until the pasta is done to your taste, stirring frequently. Remove and sprinkle grated cheese over individual servings.

Serves 6–8.

Green Pea, Broccoli, and Potato Soup
Zuppe di Piselli, Broccoli, e Patate

You will need:

½ cup	extra virgin olive oil	1 pkg	(10 oz) frozen green peas
1	medium onion, diced	1 lb	diced potatoes
3	stalks celery, chopped	3	quarts Chicken Broth
2 cups	broccoli crowns		(see page 66)
	and stalks, chopped	¼ lb	spaghettini, broken small
1 tbsp	dried basil		grated Romano cheese
1 tsp	oregano		

salt and pepper to taste

Preparation:

Combine oil, onion, celery, and broccoli in a 6-quart pot and simmer 10 minutes. Add basil, oregano, and salt and pepper, then simmer 5 minutes. Add frozen peas and potatoes and simmer for another 15 minutes, stirring frequently to be sure the potatoes don't stick.

Add the broth, bring to a boil, and reduce heat. Cook for another 30 minutes, or until the potatoes begin to get tender. Add the broken spaghettini and let slow-boil another 15 minutes, or until pasta is done. Remove and let sit 10–15 minutes. Serve sprinkled with cheese.

Serves 6.

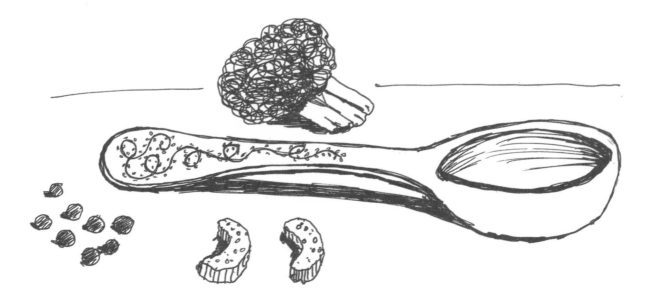

Sicilian Split Pea Soup
Zuppe Siciliana di Piselli

You will need:

1 lb	green split peas		1 tsp	dried basil
3 quarts	Beef or Chicken Broth (see page 66)		½ tsp	tarragon
4 tbsp	extra virgin olive oil			salt and pepper to taste
1 cup	celery, chopped		1½ cups	potatoes, diced
1 cup	carrots, diced		6	slices of toasted Italian bread
½ cup	green onion, chopped			grated Romano cheese

Preparation:

Rinse peas under running water, checking for possible stones. Add peas to the broth in a medium saucepan, bring to a boil, and then reduce to a simmer. The peas will be cooking while you prepare the other vegetables.

Heat olive oil in a 6-quart pot, then simmer the onions, celery, and carrots. Add the basil, tarragon, and salt and pepper. Simmer 10 minutes, then add the potatoes. Cover and cook 15 minutes, stirring to prevent the vegetables from sticking. Add the peas and broth from the saucepan. Lower heat to a simmer and cook until peas are tender and soup is thick.

Serve the stew in individual bowls, over slices of toasted bread. Sprinkle with the cheese.

Serves 6.

On Dieting Without Hunger

THE OLD MAN was once called upon to be best man at a wedding, but found that the formal dinner jacket and pants he owned had drastically shrunk after years of storage with too many mothballs. This is an invariable consequence even when the most expensive mothballs are used. Rather than take up an argument with the local mothball dealer, my father decided to reduce his own girth and thus outfox the villain.

Far from eating less, he simply took to cooking himself each night a stew of vegetables or fish, and eating all he wished. This was usually a monstrously huge bowlful with golden grated cheese floating on top. There was always enough to afford all of us a plateful as well. The amazing thing was the constant variation of the menu. For though he cooked for weeks, there was never a need to repeat a dish unless one wished to.

Most of these dishes were made up on the spot. In fact, he called all of the dishes *ciambotte* (cabbage stew), without trying for further elegance. Nevertheless, they were wonderful, soul-satisfying inventions. (And yes, they were even practical.)

The suit fit fine, though a little loosely, at the wedding.

So much, then, for the complex and extravagant diets after which modern sophisticates chase. They will chase in vain until, exhausted and disillusioned and tired of tilting at obscure windmills, they return to basics: rich, glorious soup—the abiding truth in a world filled with deceptive abstractions. It nourishes mind, heart, and soul, and it also avoids the needless expense of buying two dinner jackets.*

Before offering the other recipes, I offer a sample *ciambotte* which uses a head of cabbage as a starting point. You will also notice that garlic and olive oil are near-obligatory to these affairs. The two go a long way in convincing the stomach that it has had something more nutritious than flavored water.

---

*Of course, there was the problem that his other suits were then too large. (You might have noticed that we live in an imperfect world.) The Old Man solved this problem by packing all of them in mothballs for a few weeks.

Cabbage Stew
CIAMBOTTE

Some purists will advise you to cook the pasta separately and thus avoid the starch getting into the stew. I do not advise doing this. My motive is simple: I don't intend to lose anything.

You will need:

4 tbsp	extra virgin olive oil	2	potatoes, diced
4	cloves garlic, minced	I quart	Chicken Broth
I	onion, sliced		(see page 66)
I tbsp	oregano	I can	(15 oz) butter beans, drained
I	head cabbage, coarsely chopped	I can	(15 oz) Great Northern beans,
I cup	chopped celery leaves and ends		drained
I tbsp	salt	½ cup	elbow or small shell macaroni
I tsp	pepper		grated Romano cheese

Preparation:

Heat olive oil in a large pot, then sauté the garlic and onion, stirring, until onions are translucent. Add the oregano, and then stir in the chopped cabbage. Cover the pot and simmer until the cabbage has been cooked down to half. Add celery and salt and pepper, and simmer another 5 minutes. Add potatoes and simmer 5 minutes more, stirring so potatoes do not stick to the bottom of the pot. Now add the broth.

Reduce heat and cook about 10 minutes before adding the 2 cans of beans. Bring heat back to a simmer, and stir in the macaroni. Cook about 20 minutes more until the macaroni is done and the potatoes are tender.

Spoon the *ciambotte* into large bowls, and grate cheese directly onto each serving.

Serves 6–8.

Variation: Obviously, many additional or alternative ingredients may be added or used in this recipe. A few chopped tomatoes, for example, can be tossed in. Carrots and string beans are good, as are turnips or rutabaga instead of potatoes. You may want a richer flavor, which can be achieved with a spoonful of sugar. On the other hand, a squeeze of lemon or vinegar will give the dish tartness. Follow your taste buds and your inclinations, and you may find happiness.

Chicken Cacciatore
POLLO ALLA CACCIATORE

"Alla cacciatora" means "hunter style." The recipe that follows is more primitive and thereby more original than the cacciatore dish found in most restaurants. The latter is nearly always a few pieces of chicken served with a tomato sauce. To call it *cacciatore* is a shameful fraud, and probably due to the corrupting French influence on our cuisine.

You will need:

1 cup	extra virgin olive oil	2 tbsp	oregano
1 cup	all-purpose flour (for dredging)	½ cup	fresh, chopped basil leaves (or 2 tbsp dried)
1	large fryer, 3½–4 lbs, cut up	salt and pepper to taste	
4	cloves garlic, thinly sliced		
2	medium onions, diced	6 cups	tomato sauce (see page 102)
½ lb	carrots, cut bite-size	1 pkg	(10 oz) frozen green peas
2 lbs	potatoes, peeled and cut bite-size	½ lb	zucchini, cut bite-size
		½ cup	red wine

Preparation:

Put half the olive oil in a large skillet and bring to medium heat. Flour chicken parts and flash fry them to a golden brown. Transfer chicken to a covered bowl. Don't discard the oil and drippings—they'll add to the flavor of the sauce.

If you're using prepared tomato sauce, combine it with the oil and drippings. If preparing the tomato sauce now, use the same pan in which you fried the chicken and cook the sauce for only half an hour or so. (It will finish cooking in the oven.)

Preheat oven to 375°. Pour remaining olive oil into a large baking pan with a cover, and add garlic and onions. (At every stage the pan should be covered.) Cook for 5 minutes. Add carrots and cook 10 minutes more. Add potatoes, oregano, and basil. Salt and pepper the mixture liberally and stir well so that potatoes are coated with oil. Bake a further 15–20 minutes, stirring once or twice.

Add the chicken to the mixture and bake about 5 minutes. Then stir in the tomato sauce, peas, and zucchini. Bake for a final 45 minutes, stirring 3 or 4 times. Add wine to thin the sauce as it thickens. Test the potatoes with a fork after about 35 minutes, and continue baking until they break apart. Remove pan from oven and let it sit at least 15 minutes.

Serves 6-8.

Note: Some recipes suggest parboiling the potatoes to ensure that they will be cooked and tender. I do not recommend this. Too often the potatoes remain bland and tasteless because they absorbed the boiling water rather than the sauce during the cooking process.

THE NAME CACCIATORE comes naturally to this tasty invention. Picture a small group of friends trouping across their neighbors' farms in the fall, hunting for small game. What could be more natural than pocketing a few unharvested potatoes and tomatoes, perhaps an onion or two, possibly even a chicken? This last in extremis—and only because there are no rabbits to be shot. This is just as well, since the hunters have brought along some wine to ward off the chill and are too jovial to murder gentle, furry little things. With a chicken it is different. Chickens are arrogant, bad-tempered, smelly little despots who are valuable only when they are dead. In the middle of such a fine afternoon, how pleasant to put a large pot over a fire and throw in the day's finds. Thus was born Chicken Cacciatore.

In this country, we would have simply called it "hobo stew." The taste would be the same, but the romance and charm would be missing.

CIOPPINO IS NOT a Sicilian dish and, in fact, is not a dish found in Italy at all. By all accounts it is native to the Fisherman's Wharf area of San Francisco, and its popularity has spread from there. That it deserves its popularity goes without question. It is a lovely and delightful feast and marks an outstanding victory for our side in the war.*

What is confounding is that its invention was a long time in coming and that it had to be originated by transplanted Italians. It underscores the constant need to revise our tactics and our plans for the future. Obviously, if such a recipe could go unnoticed for so long, there must be other stones unturned and other triumphs to be won.

---

* This is the Old Man talking. His reference to "our side in the war" has never been clear. He always referred to "the war" when he grew angry or impatient with depressing things, such as professional pessimists who minimize the enjoyment of life. Perhaps he meant pedantic fools who write cookbooks. Or, he might have been a little paranoid.

# *Fisherman's Stew*
Cioppino

In this recipe, I recommend a simple, basic set of ingredients and a mildly flavored sauce. Although many recipes call for lobster or scallops, I don't—mainly because of the outrageous price they command. But include them if you desire. They can do no harm.

I have also seen recipes that ask for chunks of fish such as cod. I do not feel this to be appropriate, if for no other reason than they are not shellfish.

Note that the clams first need to be immersed in cold water for 10 hours or overnight. Cioppino can be cooked in an 8-quart pot on top of the stove, or in a large baking pan or casserole dish in the oven. Here is the stovetop method.

You will need:

1 lb	cherrystone clams (immerse 10 hours or overnight in cold water)	2 cans	(28 oz) Italian plum tomatoes
		2 tbsp	sugar
½ cup	extra virgin olive oil	½ cup	dry white wine
4	cloves garlic, thinly sliced	2	large dungeness crabs, cleaned and sectioned
1	medium onion, chopped		
2 tbsp	oregano	1 lb	medium shrimp, shelled and deveined
salt and pepper to taste			
½ cup	fresh, chopped basil leaves (or 2 tbsp dried)	grated lemon zest	
		2–3	sprigs fresh, chopped parsley

Preparation:

Heat olive oil in a large pot and sauté the garlic and onions. Add oregano and salt and pepper. Add dried basil now, or fresh basil with the tomatoes. Simmer 10 minutes or until onions are translucent. Add tomatoes and sugar (and fresh basil), and reduce to a pulp with a masher. Add wine once the mixture comes to a slow boil. Simmer at a reduced heat for 20 minutes, stirring occasionally.

Add the crab and shrimp, and once again bring the mixture to a slow boil before reducing the heat to a simmer. Simmer for 10 minutes, or until shrimp appear opaque. Add clams and return to a boil for about 3 minutes before removing the pot from the heat. Allow the pot to stand, covered, for at least 5 minutes (longer is fine). Discard any clam shells that have not opened.

Serve on large platters with grated lemon zest and chopped parsley sprinkled on top. Serve with hot bread, cold wine, and bibs. Eat with fingers and loud sounds.

Serves 6–8.

Tomato Paste

Y OU WILL FIND that the next recipe, Stufato di Pesce, contains an ingredient, tomato paste, which is bought in cans of various sizes in our markets.

For those among our readers seeking a degree in social anthropology, I offer the information that Italians once regarded canned tomato paste as a marvel of ingenuity only to be compared to a machine that would slice bread in uniform slabs.

Before the canning process was developed, the only way to make a tomato sauce in winter was by using *conserva*. Making *conserva* took several days of back-breaking work by the women.

A long table, 20–40 feet long, was set up, and the peeled, seeded plum tomatoes were spread on the top for the sun to dry. During the day the women constantly turned over the tomatoes, so they would not stick. When the sun went down, sheets were spread over the table to keep off the insects. By the second day the amount of pulp had been reduced to one small tabletop. By the third day they were turning over a large, gooey brown mass that had nearly all the water out of it. When the mass was reduced to the size of a loaf of bread and the consistency of clay, it was *conserva*.

Olive oil was rubbed over the surface and the loaf was wrapped in cheesecloth and put in a cool closet for future use. How was it used? They would cut off a small wedge and place it in a pot with some warm water. Over a slow flame they rubbed and stirred the wedge, adding water as needed, until they ended up with the equivalent of a 6-oz. can of tomato paste.

The old ways may very well be the best ways, but the 6-oz. can of paste is the exception to that rule. So said the Old Man and, remembering the alacrity with which Italian women reached for this new device, he added, "Also, I am not a lunatic."

On the other hand, to paraphrase Mark Twain: "A certain amount of work is good for a woman. It keeps her from brooding over the fact that she's a woman."*

---

*The Old Man's sense of humor never went over well with professional feminists—or, for that matter, with professional anyones. I am willing to admit his comments are deplorable. I blush because of them, but what can I do?

Fish Stew

Stufato di Pesce

You will need:

4 tbsp	extra virgin olive oil	2 cups	Chicken Broth
1	medium onion, coarsely chopped		(see page 66)
4	celery sticks, cut bite-size	1 lb	zucchini, cut bite-size
1 lb	carrots, cut bite-size	2 lbs	fillet of firm-fleshed fish, such
handful	fresh parsley, chopped		as cod or haddock (mixed or
1 tsp	thyme		matched and cut into ¾″
1 tsp	oregano		squares)
½ tsp	tarragon	1 can	(6 oz) tomato paste
pepper to taste		½ cup	dry white wine
1 lb	potatoes, cut in ¾″ cubes	salt to taste	

Preparation:

Heat olive oil in a large pot with a tight-fitting cover. Add the onion and sauté for 5 minutes. Add celery, carrot, parsley, thyme, oregano, tarragon, and pepper. Stir and simmer until carrots are on the firm side of tender. Add the potatoes and 1 cup of the broth, and cook at medium heat for 10 minutes.

Add the zucchini and fish and stir well. Add the other cup of broth when mixture starts to simmer. Return to a simmer and cook 5 minutes more. Add the tomato paste, and stir in the wine. Taste and adjust for salt.

Simmer until the potatoes break easily with a fork and the fish is done.

Serves 6–8.

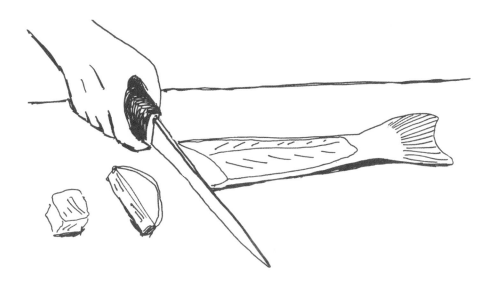

Fish Stew in a White Sauce
Stufato di Pesce alla Besciamella

You will need:

Cream sauce	
2 cups	half-and-half cream, scalded
⅛ tsp	tarragon
2	bay leaves
4 tbsp	butter
3 tbsp	all-purpose flour
¼ tsp	white pepper
salt	

Stew	
1 cup	small white boiling onions
2 cups	carrots, cut bite-size
2 cups	potatoes, cut bite-size
4 tbsp	extra virgin olive oil
1	medium onion, coarsely chopped
½ tsp	oregano
½ cup	Chicken Broth (see page 66)
1 ½ lbs	thick fish fillets (cod, halibut, red snapper, etc.), cut into 1″ chunks
salt to taste	
finely chopped parsley (for garnish)	

Preparation:

The sauce. Heat the cream in a small saucepan, then add the tarragon and bay leaves. Stir until the cream comes to a boil, then set aside. Melt the butter in a second saucepan and slowly add the flour, whisking to prevent lumps. Slowly add the cream when the mixture is smooth and continue to stir while adding the white pepper and salt. The mixture will thicken as you stir it over low heat. Set aside and proceed with the stew.

The stew. Parboil slightly the whole onions, carrots, and potatoes. Drain (they should be quite firm) and set aside. Heat olive oil in a large pot, add the chopped onion and oregano, cover the pot, and sauté for 5 minutes. Add the potatoes and carrots, but not the whole onions. Add the broth. Bring to a simmer and cook, covered, for 5 minutes.

Add the fish, whole onions, and salt. Fold the ingredients gently with a spatula. (Try not to break up the fish.) Simmer for 3 minutes, covered. Slowly add the cream sauce. Continue folding with the spatula.

Cover and simmer another 5 minutes, or until the potatoes break apart with a fork and the fish is cooked. Remove from heat. Ladle the stew into individual bowls before sprinkling with the parsley.

Serves 6.

Lamb Stew
Stufato di Agnello

You will need:

2 tbsp	extra virgin olive oil
1 ½ lbs	boneless lamb shoulder, cut into 1″ cubes
1	large onion, coarsely chopped
2 cups	Beef Broth (see page 66)
1 cup	carrots, sliced
¼ tsp	thyme

¼ tsp	marjoram
¼ tsp	mint leaves, dried
salt and pepper to taste	
3	medium potatoes, cut bite-size
1 cup	frozen peas

Preparation:

Heat olive oil in a 6-quart casserole with a tight-fitting cover. Fast-brown the lamb over moderately high heat. Lower the heat to medium, add the onion, and cook 10 minutes.

Add 1 cup of the broth and then the carrots. Cover and cook 15 minutes more. Add herbs and seasonings, and continue cooking until the carrots are nearly done. Add the potatoes, peas, and remaining broth. Simmer until the potatoes are completely cooked.

Serves 4–6.

Stewed Tripe
Stufato di Trippa

For the brave of heart. Those unaccustomed to the odor of boiling tripe are in for an unpleasant surprise.

You will need:

2 lbs	honeycomb tripe (follow instructions carefully)	2	large green bell peppers, cut into strips
3–4 tsp	salt		salt and pepper to taste
4 tbsp	extra virgin olive oil	4	large, ripe tomatoes, peeled and coarsely chopped
4	cloves garlic, minced	½ lb	small cooking onions
1	medium onion, sliced	2 tsp	sugar
2 tsp	oregano	⅛ tsp	dried red pepper, crushed
¼ tsp	tarragon		
4	stalks celery, chopped into 1″ chunks		

Preparation:

Clean and process the tripe. Wash it thoroughly, then place it in a large covered pot with 3–4 quarts salted water.

Boil the tripe for 2½–3 hours, covered. Remove from the pot and wash the tripe in cold water. Slice it into strips ¾″ wide, then cut the strips into 2″ chunks. Set aside.

Heat olive oil in a large skillet, then sauté garlic, onion, oregano, and tarragon for 5 minutes with the cover on. Stir occasionally. Add the tripe and celery and stir fry for 3 minutes.

Add the bell pepper and salt and pepper, stir-frying for another 5 minutes. Add the tomatoes, onions, and sugar, bringing the mixture to a slow simmer. Add the crushed red pepper and cover. Simmer 45 minutes. Test the tripe. It should be chewy, like soft gristle.

Serves 4–6.

Pasta and Sauces

Pasta e Sughi

HOW MANY heroes lie in forgotten stillness while far off a clamoring world sings odes to villains? It is disagreeably true that "Harry" of Agincourt and Nelson of Trafalgar are still saluted after all this time, while not the slightest remnant of memory remains of that man courageous enough to first attack the mighty artichoke.

And to what can we compare the invention of pasta? Only mankind's finest victories (the moon landing comes to mind) stand level with that golden discovery.

Ah, please, dull us not with some tawdry tale of smuggled Chinese merchandise and traveling northerners. We have long tired of that story. Pasta was our victory long before there was a Marco Polo, before there was a Venice. It even predates the Romans, for our Etruscan ancestors are known to have sung its praises.

Friends, whenever you find yourself behind a bowl of *Linguine in Bianco alle Vongole* or about to stab a succulent *Ravioli con Ripieno di Ricotta o Manzo*, I urge you to bow reverently. At the very least you might manage to mumble a small *"ave"* around your mouthful of *mostaccioli*.

Here is something quite droll. We never ate spaghetti in our home. We ate linguine or fettuccine or rigatoni or ziti or perhaps a hundred other kinds of pasta, but not spaghetti. We found the texture somewhat coarse and the taste too bland. Now, since the pasta dough is always the same and only the shape changes, there will be some pretentious iconoclast who insists that it is nonsense to prefer one type of pasta over another.

Let that fool consider whether he prefers roast ham, sliced paper-thin and piled gently into a sandwich—or the same amount of ham, cut in one thick slab and slapped between two chunks of bread!

There are so many fools in this world—and have you noticed how talkative they are?

Well, let us move on to the making of pasta. We will start with a recipe for the homemade pasta dough and see where it leads us.

Note: We've estimated about one pound of pasta for four servings. Of course, some sauces are heavier than others. And some appetites are healthier.

Egg Noodle Dough
Pasta all'Uovo

This recipe will yield about 8 ounces of dough and can be used to make any type of pasta you wish, provided you want the dough to be yellow. If you wish to make a green or a red pasta, you need only add about 4 ounces of chopped spinach or precooked, pulverized beets and leave one egg out of the recipe.

Eight ounces of dough should feed two people, unless they are really hungry.

You will need:

2 cups	all-purpose flour	1	egg yolk, also beaten
½ tsp	salt	2 tbsp	extra virgin olive oil
3	eggs, well beaten (if mixing dough by machine, leave out 1 egg)		

Preparation:

Sift salt into flour. Mix whole eggs and added egg yolk with the oil, and add to flour. Mix with a fork or your fingers, then transfer to a floured board. Knead for at least 10 minutes, or until dough is smooth and elastic. Place in a bowl and cover for 30 minutes.

To shape the dough by hand, divide it into four parts and roll out each as thinly as possible. Cut into lengths about 4″ wide and 12″ long, then roll each length into a jelly-roll shape. Slice ¼″ from the end of the roll and continue slicing off ¼″ sections until you have used up the roll. Unroll each section into a strip, then lay out the strips to dry.

The pasta can be cooked immediately, but will cook very quickly—5–7 minutes—so be ready.

You can certainly freeze this dough. But if you're keeping it in the refrigerator, remember you've used raw eggs, so a couple of days are maximum.

Serves 2 moderately hungry people.

I HAVE HEARD that at Easter time in Sicily, some people will make a black pasta by using the ink from an octopus. I have never seen this done, although I have seen some religious people make a black sauce with the ink, then throw in the delicious baby octopi to go with it. Perhaps they aren't as religious as they are hungry. I only mention the matter because I consider it curious. I do not expect anyone to try it. At least, I would not recommend it.

Y OU ARE now an expert in making homemade pasta, so it is only appropriate that I offer a couple of recipes for you to try. The first is cannelloni and the second ravioli. Cleverly spaced between these two are the cheese and meat stuffings that you'll require. Further on, we will look at other recipes that call for our stuffings. Those recipes, however, use dry, commercial pasta. The homemade type cooks quickly! The commercial stuff takes perhaps three times as long. You may consider yourself warned about this.

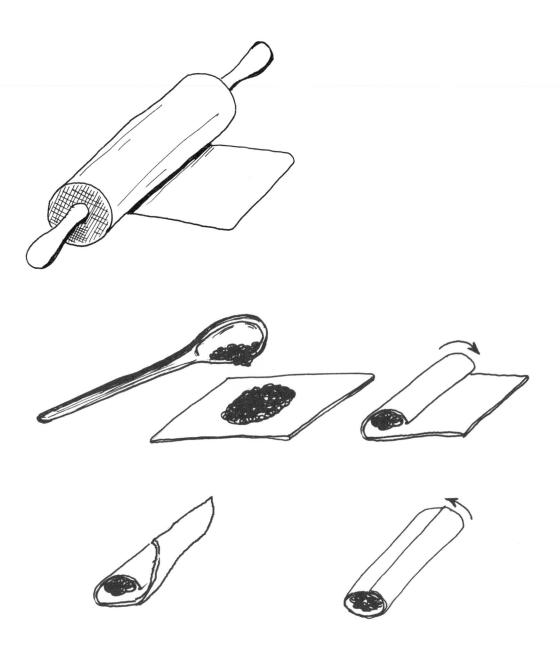

Cannelloni is a kind of homemade manicotti. The difference is that manicotti, being dry, must first be precooked. Also, stuffing the tubular manicotti takes delicate handling. Cannelloni, on the other hand, is filled and then rolled into a tubular shape. Here is how it is done:

You will need:

2	complete recipes for Egg Noodle Dough (see page 93)	1	egg white (for sealing the dough)
2	recipes for Ricotta Filling (see opposite page) *or* 1 recipe for Ricotta Filling and 1 recipe for Beef Filling (see page 98)	3 cups	Tomato Sauce with Ground Beef (see page 104)
		½ cup	mozzarella cheese, shredded
		¼ cup	grated Romano cheese

Preparation:

First, prepare the egg noodle dough, fillings, and sauce.

Roll out the dough to a thickness of ⅟16″. Trim the edges and cut the dough to form 5″ squares. Spoon 2 heaping tablespoons of filling in the center of each piece, spreading evenly. Fold one edge of dough over the filling and brush the top with egg white. Fold the other edge on top and seal. Repeat until you run out of ingredients.

Preheat oven to 375°.

Spoon at least half the sauce into the bottom of an ovenproof pan, then line the cannelloni in rows to cover the pan. *Do not piggy-back.* Sprinkle the mozzarella over the rows, followed by the rest of the sauce and then the grated Romano cheese. Cover tightly with foil and bake for 50 minutes.

Remove the pan from the oven, take off the foil, and let the cannelloni sit for 10 minutes before serving

Makes 8–10 cannelloni and can feed 6 people at least.

Variations: Once you understand how the affair is done, you will see that any number of fillings can be used, including veal, pork, chicken, and even spiced vegetables.

Ricotta Filling
Ripieno di Ricotta

This filling can be used in lasagna, manicotti, cannelloni, baked mostaccioli, baked mafalda, or jumbo shells.

You will need:

I lb	ricotta cheese		¼ tsp	pepper
¼ cup	grated Romano cheese		¼ cup	mozzarella cheese, diced
I	egg, well beaten		½ cup	fresh parsley, chopped
½ tsp	salt		½ cup	light or heavy cream (optional)

Preparation:

No cooking is required. Simply combine all the ingredients and whip until smooth. If the mixture is too dry, add some cream.

Yields 2 cups.

Gourmet Beef Filling
RIPIENO DI MANZO DEL BUONGUSTAIO

You will need:

2 tbsp	butter	1 lb	lean ground beef
4 tbsp	extra virgin olive oil	¼ lb	mushrooms, chopped
1	small onion, chopped	12	green olives, pitted and chopped
1	large green bell pepper, diced	1	tablespoon capers
1 tsp	oregano	salt and pepper to taste	
½ tsp	tarragon		

Preparation:

Heat butter and oil in a large skillet with a tight-fitting cover. Add onion and bell pepper and sauté for 5 minutes. Add oregano, tarragon, and black pepper, stirring slowly. After 5 minutes add the ground beef and cook for about 10 minutes, or until the meat is done.

Stir in the mushrooms and salt, and let simmer for a few minutes more. Remove pan from the heat, add the olives and capers, and set aside for later use.

Yields 2 cups.

Note: The mixture can be refrigerated for 3 days. It will fill about 5 dozen ravioli or 25 jumbo shells.

 # *Ravioli with Ricotta or Beef Filling*
RAVIOLI CON RIPIENO DI RICOTTA O MANZO

You will need:

2	complete recipes for Egg Noodle Dough (see page 93)		flour (for dusting)
1	complete recipe for Ricotta or Beef Filling (see pages 97 and 98)	2 tbsp	salt
		3 cups	Tomato Sauce with Ground Beef (see page 104)
1	egg white (to seal)	½ cup	grated Romano cheese

Preparation:

First, prepare the sauce and filling. Then make the egg noodle dough.

Roll out the dough to a thickness of ⅟₁₆″. Trim the edges with a cutter to form a long rectangle. Cut into 2″ squares. Spoon a teaspoon of filling in the center of each square.

Brush egg white around the edges of the square and then place another square on top, to make a package. Seal the edges with the tines of a fork. As each raviolo is finished, dust with flour to prevent sticking. Set aside.

Add salt to the water and bring to a boil in a large pot. Drop in the ravioli one by one, slowly stirring with a wooden spoon. Cook the ravioli at a slow boil for about 20 minutes, stirring occasionally. Drain very gently to avoid splitting any of the ravioli.

Serve on a large platter, with prepared sauce and grated cheese on top.

Serves 6.

Variation: A variation on the above is *agnolotti*. Using the same recipe, cut the dough into small circles and fold over the filling so the result is a half-moon shape.

The Sauce

THE SAUCE is of tomato and not to be confused with lesser sauces. Some Italians mistakenly refer to it as "the gravy" and, though the appellation unmasks their lack of sophistication, they mean no harm. Ignorance in itself is not to be despised. Churchill's father maintained it was like virginity: once lost, it could not be regained.

But let us return to the sauce. I hasten to hope the reader does not mistake me for a Frenchman because I emphasize this. The French, you know, will sweat gallons over a stove for as much as five hours and finally end up with only a sauce, which they indiscriminately pour over any inanimate object. How typical of these strange people who make war upon their food and preen themselves upon the logic of their natures.

Regarding the sauce, my sainted father was once asked why his sauce tasted more "Italian" than that of others. He answered with the old Sicilian proverb, "*Ogni fegatetu di musca sempre è sustanza,*" which loosely means, "Even in the liver of a fly there is some sustenance." Perhaps he meant by this that good cooking results from paying careful attention to all the little details. On the other hand, he may simply have been joking. He was a playful man and fond of laughter, and for this reason any recipe he wrote down was likely to contain a little joke.

But come, I wish to speak of sauce and to state that good sauce holds no great "mystery" shared by secretive chefs. It needs only that you use good ingredients and good timing, with a cheerful heart. Observe.

Use olive oil. Pure olive oil. Pure, imported olive oil. Even more, it should be extra virgin olive oil, which is the first pressing of the olive.* It is thick and green, not pale and light as with later pressings. Of course, one can make sauce by using any vegetable oil, but I would not recommend it (any more than I would recommend using 30-weight crankcase oil, which at least has the benefit of being cheap). You know, I once heard of a depraved woman of Italian ancestry living in Texas who actually used bacon drippings as a substitute for olive oil; but this is too sad a story to continue.

Use imported Greek oregano that is still on the twigs and branches and wrapped in tissue paper. The oregano sold in bottles and cans in local markets tastes like stale tea leaves by comparison. Better yet, grow your own.

Grow your own basil. If you have never tasted fresh, sweet basil just plucked from the bush, you have not truly tasted basil. Yet it grows easily and quickly from seed, transplants well, and can even be grown in the house if you have a sunny window. The dried dust you buy in markets is not the real thing, though it is probably better than nothing at all.

Use plum (or pear) tomatoes, which cost a few pennies more. The taste is worth a few pennies. Better still, grow your own. A package of seed for the *San Marzano* tomato costs less than a 28-ounce can and will supply you all summer long with rich, tart-tasting fruit that is magnificent in sauce or salad.

Add broth or a bit of the pasta's cooking water to thin out the sauce. I also suggest you add wine to the broth. You will think the better of yourself for doing so, and all those who taste your sauce will bless you and call you wonderful names and finally begin to appreciate your worth.

I understand that pecorino (Romano) cheese is produced domestically. Also, I am given to understand that it is not all that bad. I do not know, for I have never tasted it and do not intend to, but some friends who are usually trustworthy have said so. Imported pecorino is not much more expensive than the stuff produced locally. Since there is little difference in price, why should we take a chance on being disappointed?

I have a theory, you know, that you should always buy the best, and if you cannot afford the best you should buy the cheapest … or do without. If you once try the "in-between," you might grow satisfied with it. In that direction lies depravity (like the woman in Texas who uses bacon drippings in place of olive oil). I cheerfully admit that this is not much of a theory, but it is my own and it works for me and, anyway, I never claimed to be a great theoretician.

---

* If extra virgin seems a near-comic superlative, with what astonishment will the reader greet the concept of "extra, extra" virgin olive oil—a rare but very real item to be found in our markets. And who else but an Italian could have conceived such a thing?

Marinara Sauce

Salsa alla Marinara

If you have never tasted marinara sauce, prepare to be delighted. The sauce has little to do with mariners, no more than carbonara sauce has much to do with charcoal-burners or cacciatore with hunters. Sometimes, it is used with fish, but not out of necessity.

The important thing about it is its freshness. It is not a sauce that is simmered for hours until it is thick and gloomy. Marinara is cooked in 15–20 minutes at most, and tastes best when all ingredients have just been plucked from the garden. It goes well with linguine or spaghettini, and if the pasta is freshly handmade, the result is like the first day of spring.

You will need:

For 3–4 servings of pasta (about 1 lb)

4 tbsp	extra virgin olive oil	handful fresh, chopped basil leaves
4	cloves garlic, minced	salt and pepper to taste
2 lbs	plum tomatoes, blanched, skinned, and chopped (or one 28 oz can plum tomatoes)	grated Romano cheese

Preparation:

Heat olive oil in a saucepan and sauté the garlic. Throw in the tomatoes and raise the heat until they start to bubble. Add the basil and salt and pepper. Break the tomatoes with a fork, stirring the sauce occasionally.

Cook about 15–20 minutes, then pour the sauce over hot pasta. Sprinkle with freshly grated Romano cheese. You will not believe how good it is.

Serves 3–4.

Sicilian Tomato Sauce
Salsa di Pomodoro Alla Siciliana

You will need:

For 3–4 servings of pasta (about 1 lb)

⅓ cup	extra virgin olive oil			salt and pepper to taste
1 can	anchovies, drained		1 tsp	sugar (optional)
4	cloves garlic, thinly sliced		½ cup	currants or raisins
1 tbsp	fennel seeds			(plumped in hot water)
1 tbsp	oregano		½ cup	pine nuts
½ cup	red wine		1 tbsp	capers
2 cans	(28 oz) peeled		1 cup	Roasted Bread Crumbs
	plum tomatoes			(see page 60)
½ cup	fresh, chopped basil leaves			handful fresh, chopped parsley

Preparation:

Heat olive oil in a large skillet and add the anchovies, mashing with a fork until they are dissolved. Add garlic, fennel seeds, and oregano, and cook till the garlic starts to color slightly. Add wine and allow liquid to reduce by about half. Add tomatoes, breaking them up with a fork. Stir the basil into the sauce. Cover and simmer 10–15 minutes.

Taste and adjust for salt and pepper. If sauce is too tart, you can add a teaspoon of sugar. Add currants (or raisins), pine nuts, and capers. Simmer another 10–15 minutes, stirring and tasting.

Cook pasta of your choice till *al dente.* Mix half the sauce with the pasta in a serving bowl. Sprinkle some bread crumbs and the parsley over the top, and serve.

At the table, pass around the rest of the sauce and bread crumbs.

Serves: 3–4.

Tomato Sauce with Ground Beef
SALSA DI POMODORO CON MANZO MACINATO

You will need:

For 4–6 servings of pasta
(about 1 ½ lbs)

4 tbsp	extra virgin olive oil	1 lb	lean ground beef
3–4	cloves garlic, minced	1 can	(28 oz) plum tomatoes, crushed
1	small onion, finely chopped	1 can	(6 oz) tomato paste
1 tbsp	fresh, chopped basil leaves	½ cup	red wine
	(or 1 tsp dried)	½ cup	Beef Broth (see page 66)
2 tsp	oregano		sugar to taste
pepper to taste			salt to taste

Preparation:

Heat olive oil in a 4-quart saucepan, then sauté the garlic, onion, basil, oregano, and pepper until the onion is translucent. Add the beef and cook slowly until it browns. Add tomatoes and cook for 10 minutes, then add the tomato paste. Add wine and broth, then sugar and salt, adjusting for taste. Simmer ¾ hour, stirring frequently to prevent sticking.

Serves 4–6.

Meat Tomato Sauce
Salsa di Carne al Pomodoro

I suggest serving this sauce over ziti, rigatoni, or any large tubular pasta.

You will need:

**For 4-6 servings of pasta
(about 1 ½ lbs)**

4 tbsp	extra virgin olive oil		1 lb	stewing veal
4	cloves garlic, minced		2 cans	(28 oz) crushed plum tomatoes
1	onion, finely chopped		1 can	(12 oz) tomato paste
1 tbsp	oregano		½ cup	red wine
6	fresh basil leaves		1 cup	Beef Broth (see page 66)
	(or 1 ½ tsp dried basil)		2 tbsp	sugar (or to taste)
pepper to taste			salt to taste	
1 lb	lean beef ribs			
1 lb	lean pork ribs			
	(cut away excess fat)			

Preparation:

Heat olive oil in a large saucepan and add garlic, onion, oregano, basil, and pepper. Sauté until the garlic begins to color slightly. Add beef ribs, pork ribs, and veal, and sauté until the meat is almost cooked, about 20 minutes. Keep well covered.

Add the plum tomatoes to the meat mixture, stir, and simmer about 15 minutes.

Add tomato paste, wine, and broth. When the sauce starts to bubble again, add the sugar. Stir and add the salt. Lower heat to a simmer.

Simmer about 1 hour, stirring frequently so the sauce does not stick to the pan.

Drain off excess fat from the liquid. Remove meat from the sauce and, when cool enough to handle, slice or break it into chunks and return to sauce.

Serves 4–6.

Ricotta-Filled Jumbo Shells

Conchiglie Ripiene di Ricotta

You will need:

For 25–30 jumbo shells

½ cup	extra virgin olive oil		4 cups	(2 recipes) Ricotta Filling (see page 97)
6	cloves garlic, minced		½ cup	mozzarella cheese, diced into small pieces
1 can	(28 oz) crushed plum tomatoes			
½ cup	fresh, chopped basil leaves		grated Romano cheese	
salt and pepper to taste				

Preparation:

Prepare the sauce. Heat olive oil over moderate heat and add the garlic, sautéing until it starts to color slightly. Add tomatoes and, when they start to bubble, the chopped basil and salt and pepper. Stir the sauce, then lower heat and simmer 15 minutes. Cool.

Prepare ricotta filling and set aside.

Bring salted water to a rolling boil in a large pot. Drop in a few shells at a time, very carefully. When shells are all in, stir gently and bring water back to a slow boil. Cook about 10 minutes; the shells should still be firm and not fully cooked. Remove pot from the heat, pour in a cup of cold water, then place the pot under the cold-water tap. Allow the water to run slowly into the pot, until the shells have cooled. Then remove the shells by hand, a few at a time, placing them in a colander. Be careful; the shells split easily.

Mix the mozzarella cheese with the ricotta filling and fill the shells one at a time. You will find one tablespoon of the mix fits each shell nicely. There is no way to do this without making a mess. Control yourself.

Preheat oven to 375°. Pour half the sauce into a 2½″-deep baking pan, then arrange the filled shells in rows. *Do not piggy-back.* Spoon the rest of the sauce gently over the shells, then cover the pan tightly with foil. Bake for about 40 minutes.

Remove pan from the oven, take off the foil, and allow to sit 10 minutes. Sprinkle grated Romano over individual servings.

Serves 6–8.

Variation: The shells can be stuffed with meat as well as cheese. Just substitute Gourmet Beef Filling (page 98) for the Ricotta Filling.

Baked Manicotti

Manicotti al Forno

Manicotti is a dried cannelloni that has already been formed into a tube shape. It is handled and stuffed in much the same way as the jumbo shells, and can be filled with cheese or meat. The important thing is to be careful not to split the tubes.

You will need:

4 cups	(2 recipes) Ricotta Filling (see page 97)		½ cup	fresh, chopped basil leaves
½ cup	extra virgin olive oil			salt and pepper to taste
6	cloves garlic, minced		2 tbsp	extra virgin olive oil
1 can	(28 oz) crushed plum tomatoes		1 lb	manicotti
			½ cup	mozzarella cheese, diced small
				grated Romano cheese

Preparation:

Prepare the sauce. Heat olive oil over moderate heat and add the garlic, sautéing until it starts to change color. Add tomatoes and, when they start to bubble, the chopped basil and salt and pepper. Stir sauce, then lower heat and simmer 15 minutes. Set aside to cool.

Prepare the ricotta filling. Bring salted water to a rolling boil in a large pot. Add olive oil and then the manicotti, one at a time, through the floating oil, making sure the tubes are coated. (The oil prevents the tubes from sticking to one another.) Allow the water to return to a slow boil, then cook about 10 minutes. The manicotti should still be firm and not fully cooked.

Remove pot from the heat, pour in a cup of cold water to stop the cooking process, then place the pot under the cold-water tap. Allow the water to run slowly into the pot, until the pasta has cooled. Remove the manicotti by hand, a few at a time, placing them in a colander to drain.

Mix the mozzarella cheese with the ricotta filling and *carefully* fill each tube. You will find it's easiest to fill half the tube from one end before switching to the other.

Preheat oven to 375°. Pour half the sauce into a 2½″-deep baking pan, then arrange the manicotti in rows. *Do not piggy-back.* Spoon the rest of the sauce gently over the manicotti, then cover the pan tightly with foil. Bake for about 40 minutes.

Remove pan from the oven, take off the foil, and allow to sit 10 minutes. Sprinkle grated Romano over individual servings.

Serves 4–6.

Baked Mostaccioli with Tomato Sauce and Cheese
Mostaccioli al Forno alla Pizzaiola

Mostaccioli, often called penne, is a tubular pasta, the ends of which are cut diagonally so as to resemble an old-fashioned quill pen. The pasta also looks like one side of a trim mustache; hence, the title of *mostaccioli.*

You will need:

1	recipe Marinara Sauce (see page 102)	½ lb	mozzarella cheese, shredded
1 lb	mostaccioli or penne	½ cup	grated Romano cheese

Preparation:

Prepare the marinara sauce and set it aside.

Bring salted water to a rolling boil in a large pot. Add the pasta. Cook about 10–12 minutes. The pasta should be firm and not fully cooked.

Remove the pasta from the heat, pour in a cup of cold water to stop the cooking process, then place the pot under the cold-water tap. Allow the water to run slowly into the pot, until the pasta has cooled. Drain well, then transfer to a large mixing bowl.

Preheat oven to 375°.

Mix half the sauce into the pasta until evenly distributed. Spoon a little sauce into a 3″-deep baking pan, then pour half the pasta-sauce mixture evenly into the pan. Sprinkle half the mozzarella over the top.

Layer the remaining pasta-sauce mixture on top, followed by the remaining mozzarella, the balance of the tomato sauce, and the grated Romano cheese. Cover the pan tightly with foil and bake for 30 minutes.

Remove pan from the oven, take off the foil, and allow to sit 10 minutes before serving.

Serves 4.

Lasagna, Palermo Style

LASAGNE ALLA PALERMITANA

You will need:

4 cups	(2 recipes) Ricotta Filling (see page 97)	3 tbsp	extra virgin olive oil
1	recipe Tomato Sauce with Ground Beef (see page 104)	1 lb	lasagna noodles
		1 lb	mozzarella cheese, shredded
		1 cup	grated Romano cheese

Preparation:

Prepare the ricotta filling and the tomato sauce with ground beef, then set aside.

Bring salted water to a rolling boil in a large pot, then add the oil (it helps keep the pasta from sticking). Slide the lasagna noodles one at a time through the oil, crisscrossing them to avoid sticking. Let the water return to a slow boil, stir the lasagna gently, and cook about 10 minutes. The noodles should still be firm and not fully cooked.

Remove the pot from the heat, then pour in a cup of cold water to stop the cooking process. Do not drain. Instead, gently scoop out the lasagna a few handfuls at a time and place the noodles in a colander. (If you drain the lasagna all at once, you will be sorry—and will probably blame me for your troubles.)

Preheat oven to 375°.

Lasagna is built in layers. Spoon a little sauce into a pan that's at least 3″ deep and about 10″ by 14″, then arrange the first layer of noodles. Crowd them a little. Now spoon a layer of the meat sauce. Next, sprinkle both the mozzarella and the Romano. Layer another set of noodles. This time use the ricotta filling to spread on top of the pasta. Continue in this manner. All will be well if you plan ahead so that you end with a layer of meat sauce and cheeses on the top. Cover the pan tightly with foil and bake for 45 minutes.

Remove pan from the oven and let it sit, uncovered, for at least 15–20 minutes before trying to cut into this thing. The longer you let the lasagna sit, the easier it will be to cut it into squares.

Serves 4–6.

Variation: Use mafalda in place of lasagna. Because the noodle is smaller, the texture is finer. (To be frank, we always used mafalda, never lasagna, for this dish. You may be somewhat amazed at this confession, but frankness (in small doses) can be charming. I will also admit that I detest pizza (which is Neapolitan anyway). Make what you will of it.)

THE OLD MAN went shopping every Saturday morning, usually making a day of it. He would take one of his children with him to guard his purchases while he sought out new "battles." The vegetable sellers would quake when they saw him. One vendor of tomatoes, I recall, insisted that no one touch the fruit unless he bought first. So the Old Man "bought" several pounds and then spilled the bag's contents, looking through them one by one. He rejected nearly half as unworthy and demanded substitutes before he would pay. Food—the getting as well as the cooking and eating—was his delight.

Lesser Sauces

IT IS NOT my wish to provoke an argument, but anyone who associates pasta exclusively with tomato sauce is a fool who lacks experience, education, and imagination.

To prove my assertion, I offer the following multi-colored (yellow, green, white, and black) creations that, when used in moderation with pasta, will do no lasting harm.

Now you can, of course, simply pour melted butter over hot pasta and declare it a "yellow sauce." However, I prefer the wonderfully primitive Olio e Aglio as a better example—though I hasten to warn that you should have a liking for garlic and olive oil, for there is little else you will taste in the affair.

The other sauces—green, white, and black—follow in quick order. In all honesty, I must admit they are not particularly Sicilian, but they are included here because they taste good.

Oil and Garlic Sauce
SUGO OLIO E AGLIO

You will need:

For 1–2 servings of pasta

½ cup   extra virgin olive oil

4   cloves garlic, minced

handful fresh, coarsely chopped parsley

salt and pepper to taste

grated Romano cheese

1 tsp   crushed red pepper (optional)

Preparation:

Heat olive oil in a saucepan, then sauté the garlic for 3–5 minutes. Just before the garlic browns, toss in the parsley and salt and pepper. Stir for about 1 minute. Remove pan from heat.

Pour the sauce over hot pasta, then sprinkle grated cheese over each serving. For those with discriminating palates, sprinkle on a bit of the crushed red pepper as well.

Serves 1–2.

Basil Sauce
PESTO

You see, the easiest and cheapest way to make a green sauce is to use parsley. If you have a blender and a little garlic and olive oil, you can whip out a sparkling green paste that can be thinned with broth or even some of the hot water in which you cook the pasta. But if you are truly serious about this and if cost is no object, pesto is the way to go.

Pesto is green and is as fine a way to treat basil as can be found within a thousand miles in any direction from Genoa.

You will need:

2 cups	fresh basil	1 cup	freshly grated Romano cheese
2	cloves garlic	⅔ cup	extra virgin olive oil
½ cup	pine nuts		

Preparation:

Use a food processor or blender to whip the basil, garlic, and pine nuts into a paste. Add the cheese and olive oil, a little at a time. Freeze or refrigerate, with a thin layer of olive oil covering the sauce as a seal.

Bring the pesto to room temperature before using. It works well with pasta, in soups or salads, or even as a spread.

Serves 3–4.

PESTO IS ESSENTIALLY a way of storing basil over the winter. Another way to store it is to clean and wipe dry the leaves and then salt them down in layers in large jars. Olive oil is poured over each layer and over the top as a seal. (The leaves sometimes turn black, but this still beats the dried stuff.)

Endless variations of the sauce can be discovered throughout the Mediterranean, with a bit of mint added here and a handful of walnuts there. But authentic pesto is from Genoa, and that is the end of the argument. Though northern, the Genoese are similar to Sicilians in their affinity for good cooking, love of pastry, and distaste for pork. This reflects the Arab influence so noted in the south. I know of a second-hand Genoese (a Californian) who mistakenly thought his dislike for ham was a matter of personal taste, whereas it was pure and simple heritage.

Fettuccine with White Cream Sauce

Fettuccine all'Alfredo

Alfredo is a white cream sauce and is Roman in origin. It is nearly as simple to make as Olio e Aglio, and it is included here to demonstrate the lengths to which I will go to win a minor argument. Actually it does not taste bad and, if used in moderation, can do you no harm.

You will need:

For 2–3 servings of fettuccine

1 cup	butter
1 tbsp	fresh, finely chopped parsley
salt and pepper to taste	

1 cup	light cream
1 cup	Parmesan cheese, grated

Preparation:

Melt butter in a medium saucepan over a low flame. Add the parsley and salt and pepper. Stir for a minute and add the cream. Bring to a slow simmer, then cook and stir for another minute before folding in the cheese. Remove from heat after a minute.

Pour sauce over hot fettuccine.

Serves 2–3.

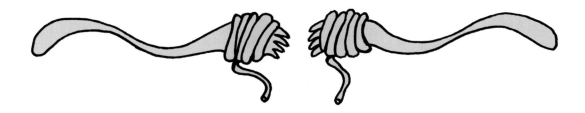

Seafood Sauces

HERE ARE SOME fine recipes well worth knowing. Anchovy sauce will come as a pleasant surprise, even for those foolish enough to dislike the anchovy taste. You will find the sauce is not gritty or salty; instead, it is a smooth, mild, and delightful repast.

I have included both red and white clam sauce. (No one is such a boor as to dislike clams. I say this, confident that I shall not offend the reader, since no one who has read this far could possibly be a boor.)

I will even throw in a recipe for mussel sauce. I do this because, even though very similar to red clam sauce, mussel sauce is so particularly fine a taste that it deserves a special mention all its own.

And what of black sauces? As you might have guessed, a black sauce is made by combining several ingredients with the ink of squid, cuttlefish, octopus, or some such creature. Octopus is the best candidate in this affair. The difficulty here is one must find fresh octopus with the ink sac intact. Most markets sell the little animal distressingly clean. However, should you succeed, the octopus is boiled for nearly an hour with olive oil, tomatoes, oregano, rosemary, and parsley. The ink is then stirred in, and the sauce, octopus and all, is poured over the hot pasta. It is not a dish I feel comfortable in recommending.

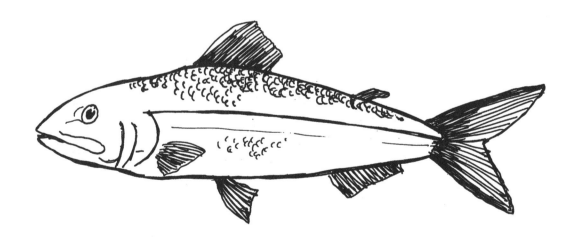

Anchovy Sauce
SALSA DI ACCIUGHE

A thin noodle like spaghettini is best for this sauce. The traditional bread crumb topping takes the place of cheese, which is usually salty. Also, this topping is much cheaper than cheese—something that has probably already occurred to you.

You will need:

For 4–6 servings
of pasta (about 1 ½ lbs)

2 cups	coarse bread crumbs, browned in ¼ cup extra virgin olive oil	3	fresh mint leaves, minced
		pepper	to taste
¼ cup	extra virgin olive oil	1 can	anchovies, drained
3	cloves garlic, thinly sliced	2 tbsp	capers
1 lb	plum tomatoes, peeled and chopped	½ cup	sliced black olives, pitted
		1 cup	fresh, coarsely chopped parsley
handful	fresh, chopped basil leaves	salt	to taste

Preparation:

Brown bread crumbs in ¼ cup olive oil and set aside. Heat another ¼ cup of olive oil in a wide saucepan, then add the garlic and, before it browns, the tomatoes. Add the basil, mint, and pepper when the mixture begins to bubble. Simmer for 20 minutes, while the pasta is cooking.

Mash anchovies into a paste, combine with capers and olives, and stir into the sauce. Allow sauce to simmer until it is again hot, then stir in the parsley. Taste for salt. Remove sauce from stove after about 3 minutes. Mix it gently into the hot pasta. Sprinkle the browned bread crumbs over individual servings.

Serves 4–6.

Variations: There are several variations on this recipe, and in many of them Sicilians tend to make the meal sweet rather than salty. They will add sweet red peppers to the sauce and sometimes even sugar to the bread crumbs. I have always felt that salt is a proper taste and needs no apology or disguise.

Pasta with Fresh Anchovies
PASTA ALLE ALICI FRESCHE

This meal takes a little time to prepare, but the results are well worth the effort. If fresh anchovies are not available, other fish, such as sardines or smelts, can be substituted. The cleaning of fish is the same. Remove the head, tail, and backbone. Then slice the fish lengthwise in half. Much of the meat will disintegrate in cooking, making a thick sauce, but the taste will be mild.

You will need:

For 4 servings (1 lb) of pasta
(mostaccioli is best)

1½ lbs	fresh anchovies (or a substitute, such as fresh sardines or fresh smelts)	1 cup	Chicken Broth (see page 66)
⅔ cup	extra virgin olive oil		salt to taste
3	cloves garlic, minced		juice of 1 lemon
1 lb	plum tomatoes, skinned and chopped	½ cup	fresh, chopped parsley
			grated Romano cheese
			hot red pepper, crushed (optional)

Preparation:

Cook pasta until al dente. Clean the anchovies (or other fish), wash in salt water, and dry on paper towels. Preheat oven to 375°.

Heat olive oil, then sauté the garlic for 3–5 minutes (don't let it brown). Throw in the tomatoes, bring to a boil, and cook 5 minutes. Add broth and salt. Return to a boil, then lower heat and simmer 10 minutes.

Add fish and simmer another 5 minutes. Remove pan from the heat and squeeze in the lemon juice. Sprinkle the parsley on top.

Pour the sauce and cooked pasta into a baking dish, mixing gently and topping with grated cheese. Place in the preheated oven for 5 minutes before serving, then pass around the crushed red pepper.

Serves 4.

Note: Passing around the hot pepper gives those with allergies a chance to say no.

Pasta with Sardines
PASTA CON SARDE

Truly, one cannot speak of pasta and fish to Sicilians without coming to Pasta con Sarde, which always provokes an argument. This is because we dislike the dish. It is heavy and salty and has an odd taste, probably because the pasta is cooked in vegetable water.

Now, I could have kept still about it and set down the recipe, and my quiet reserve would have been quite admirable, in an English sort of way.

You may try this if you wish. I shall say no more about it. Except this: some Sicilians even throw raisins and pine nuts into this. Amazing!

You will need:

For 4 servings of short, stubby pasta (like rigatoni), about 1 lb

1	head fennel (finocchio)	1 lb	fresh sardines, deboned, cleaned, and washed in salt water
1 cup	extra virgin olive oil		
3	cloves garlic, thinly sliced	1 can	anchovies, drained
2	medium onions, finely chopped	salt and pepper to taste	

Preparation:

In the same pot in which you will cook the pasta, boil the fennel for 10 minutes. Save the water for cooking the pasta. Remove fennel and chop it coarsely.

Heat half the olive oil in a saucepan, then sauté the garlic and onions. Add half the sardines, mashing them into a paste. Add anchovies and chopped fennel. Cover pan and simmer until anchovies melt into the sauce. Add salt and pepper to taste.

Heat the remaining olive oil in a skillet, then fry the rest of the sardines, turning them once—carefully, to avoid breaking them. Remove whole sardines with a slotted spoon and set aside. Pour the frying oil into the sauce.

Preheat oven to 375°.

Cook the pasta until al dente, then drain. Mix half the sauce with the pasta. Layer the bottom of a casserole dish with some of the pasta-sauce mixture, then a few of the fried sardines, and then some sauce. Repeat layers until all ingredients are used up, ending up with the pasta-sauce layer. Cover and bake for 20 minutes.

It cannot poison you, no matter the taste.

Serves 4 very brave people.

Red Clam Sauce

Salsa Rossa alle Vongole

Linguine, fettuccine, or spaghetti work well in this recipe.

You will need:

For 3–4 servings of pasta (about 1 lb)

2 lbs	fresh clams (see directions below for preparing) or one 10 oz can baby clams (save the liquid)		1 ½ lbs	plum tomatoes, peeled and chopped (or one 28 oz can crushed tomatoes)
½ cup	extra virgin olive oil		1 can	(6 oz) tomato paste
4	cloves garlic, minced		½ cup	sweet vermouth
1	medium onion, finely chopped		½ cup	Chicken Broth (see page 66)
1 tbsp	oregano		1 tsp	sugar
1 tbsp	fresh, chopped basil leaves (or one tsp dried)		salt to taste	
pepper to taste			1 tsp	fresh, chopped parsley
			grated Romano cheese	

Preparation:

Preparing the clams. Be sure the clams are fresh and well scrubbed, then place them in a bowl of cold water for at least 2–3 hours.

Place clams in a saucepan with ½ cup water. Cover tightly and steam until the shells open. (Throw out any clams that do not open.) Remove the shells and extract the meat. Filter the clam juice through a cheesecloth to remove any sand, saving liquid for the sauce.

The sauce. Heat olive oil in a saucepan and sauté garlic, onion, oregano, basil, and pepper until the onion turns translucent. Add the chopped tomatoes, simmering 15 minutes until they break down. Add tomato paste, vermouth, broth, sugar, and salt.

Return to a simmer, then add the clam juice but not the clams (they will toughen if added now). Simmer another 10–15 minutes while the pasta is cooking. Add the clams, leaving the pan on the stove just long enough for them to heat.

Pour the sauce over the cooked pasta, sprinkling parsley and grated cheese on top.

Serves 3–4.

White Clam Sauce

SALSA BIANCA ALLE VONGOLE

You will need:

For 4 servings of linguine or fettuccine (about 1 lb)

3 lbs	fresh clams or two 10 oz cans baby clams (save the juice)			pepper to taste
4 tbsp	extra virgin olive oil		½ cup	dry white wine
1	small onion, finely chopped		1 ½ cups	Chicken Broth (see page 66)
4	cloves garlic, minced		½ tsp	thyme
1 tbsp	oregano			salt to taste
1 tsp	dried basil		½ cup	fresh, chopped parsley
¼ tsp	marjoram (optional)			grated Romano cheese

Preparation:

Prepare the clams. (See instructions on the opposite page.)

Heat olive oil in a saucepan, then sauté the garlic, onion, herbs, and pepper. Add the wine when the onions turn translucent. Cover and simmer 5 minutes while the wine begins to evaporate. Add the broth, clam juice (but not the clams—they'll toughen if you add them too soon), thyme, and salt, and allow to simmer.

Cook the pasta in a large pot for about 10 minutes. Just before it is fully cooked, transfer it to a colander to drain.

Pour clams (fresh or canned) into the sauce and remove pan from the heat. Return the pasta to the pasta pot, then pour the sauce with clams over the pasta. Mix thoroughly. Allow the pasta to finish cooking over low heat (it will take only a few minutes), mixing frequently to keep it from sticking.

Pour the mixture into a large serving bowl before the sauce is completely absorbed into the pasta. Sprinkle parsley on top and serve with grated Romano cheese.

Serves 4.

Scallops, Mariner's Style
COZZE ALLA MARINARA

This recipe and the following two call for cooking shellfish in a marinara sauce. There are some small variations in preparing the sauce, but the basics are the same. Still, a small variation in a recipe can account for a large difference in taste.

I recommend that the pasta used should match the sauce. For example, a crab sauce is delicate, since the meat is always flaked, so you should match it with a delicate pasta like vermicelli. On the other hand, the scallops and shrimp are lumpy and would go best with a shell macaroni or an appropriate short, stubby type like ziti or rigatoni.

But I do not wish to interfere with your eating habits or dictate terms to your conscience. Feel free to experiment in any way you choose. I know from experience that each seeks salvation by his own path. Some find it in good food. Others leave Los Angeles.

You will need:

For 3–4 servings of
ziti or rigatoni (about 1 lb)

4 tbsp	extra virgin olive oil	1 tbsp	oregano
2	cloves garlic, minced		salt and pepper to taste
1	medium onion, finely chopped	1 lb	scallops (sea scallops look best,
2 lbs	plum tomatoes, peeled and		but bay scallops also work well)
	chopped (or one 28 oz can		handful fresh, chopped parsley
	crushed tomatoes)		grated Romano cheese

Preparation:

Heat olive oil in a saucepan, then sauté the garlic and onion. Add tomatoes when the onion turns translucent, then bring to a boil and add the oregano and salt and pepper. Lower heat and simmer, covered, for 20 minutes.

Add scallops and continue simmering until they are tender, about 5 minutes. Stir in fresh parsley. Remove from heat and serve over hot pasta. Sprinkle grated cheese on top.

Serves 3–4.

Shrimp, Mariner's Style

GAMBERI ALLA MARINARA

You will need:

For 3–4 servings of
ziti or rigatoni (about 1 lb)

4 tbsp	extra virgin olive oil	6	fresh basil leaves
2	cloves garlic, minced		salt and pepper to taste
1	medium onion, finely chopped	1 lb	shrimp, shelled, deveined,
2 lbs	plum tomatoes, peeled and		and cleaned
	chopped (or one 28 oz can		grated Romano cheese
	crushed tomatoes)	¼ tsp	crushed red pepper (optional)
1 tbsp	oregano		

Preparation:

Heat olive oil in a saucepan, then sauté the garlic and onion. Add tomatoes when the onion turns translucent, then bring to a boil and add the oregano, basil, and salt and pepper. Lower heat and simmer 20 minutes, covered, stirring occasionally. Add the shrimp and cook until opaque (only a few minutes, or they will get tough).

Pour the sauce over hot pasta and sprinkle with cheese. Some people like red pepper with this dish. If you wish, add it now.

Serves 3-4.

YEARS AGO IN New York, I would take pleasure in spending summer nights fishing and crabbing from the big rocks on the Hudson up near Spuyten Duyvil or under the bridge. When the tide came in, so did the crabs, and I would fill many a basket with the lovely devils. Now, it was plainly sporting to throw back the baby bluepoint crabs, since they had little enough meat on them. It was also illegal to keep them. However, it was night, and no one was looking. Those little crabs, cleaned and delegged, performed miracles for red or white clam sauce. This is a secret (and also illegal), so if asked, I would deny ever doing such a thing.

Crab, Mariner's Style
GRANCHI ALLA MARINARA

You will need:

For 3–4 servings (about 1 lb) of a delicate pasta such as vermicelli, angel hair, or spaghettini

1	cooked crab, flaked and picked over	3–4	fresh, chopped basil leaves
4 tbsp	extra virgin olive oil		salt and pepper to taste
2	cloves garlic, minced	4 tbsp	dry white wine
½ cup	green onions, chopped		handful fresh, chopped parsley
2 lbs	plum tomatoes, peeled and chopped (or one 28 oz can crushed tomatoes)	½	lemon, squeezed
			grated Romano cheese

Preparation:

Prepare the crab (see note below).

Heat olive oil in a saucepan, then sauté the garlic and green onion. Add tomatoes and bring to a boil, then lower heat to a simmer. Add basil and salt and pepper and simmer 15–20 minutes.

Add the wine and simmer 5 minutes. Add the crab and parsley, stirring gently. When the crab is warm, squeeze in the lemon juice and remove pan from the heat. Mix gently into the pasta, and sprinkle grated cheese on top.

Serves 3–4.

Note: Seafood stores and large markets sell crab already cooked. You probably can get the fishmonger to clean the crab. To prepare it yourself: (1) Snap off the legs and claws. These you will crack with a mallet. (2) Only the two muscle structures of the body need to be broken into by hand—and here the meat is in flakes. Don't try to dismantle the muscles completely. Just flake off the edges and pick away the shell bits that are exposed. (The job is easier after the crab's been warmed in the sauce.)

Mussel Sauce
SALSA DI COZZE

Mussel sauce with fettuccine or tagliatelle—or nearly any other kind of pasta—is beautiful. The taste is soft and creamy, and the color of the cooked mussel in its shell is a pearl gold. Naturally, you will be using only fresh mussels.

You will need:

For 3-4 servings of pasta (about 1 lb)

2 lbs	mussels	salt and pepper to taste
½ cup	extra virgin olive oil	1 cup Chicken Broth (see page 66)
3	cloves garlic, minced	handful fresh, chopped parsley
4–5	plum tomatoes, peeled and	grated Romano cheese
	chopped	crushed red pepper (optional)

Preparation:

Clean and beard the mussels; soak them in cold, salted water for at least 1 hour; and then start the pasta cooking.

For the rest you will need two large pots. In the first pot, heat ¼ cup oil and sauté ⅔ of the minced garlic. Throw in the tomatoes before the garlic browns, along with the salt and pepper, and simmer for about 15 minutes or until the tomatoes have broken down.

Meanwhile, heat the remaining oil in the second pot and sauté the rest of the minced garlic. Pour in the chicken broth before the garlic browns, and bring to a simmer.

Drain the water from the mussels and carefully place them in the chicken broth (pot #2). Cover and steam 4–5 minutes, shaking the pot occasionally. Remove from heat when the shells open. (If any do not open, throw them out without compunction—as soldiers who have betrayed their trust.) Drain the stock into a bowl, reserving it. Transfer the mussels to a bowl and remove flesh from about ¾ of them, leaving the rest intact.

Pour the chicken stock into the simmering tomatoes (pot #1) and stir, allowing it to cook 5 minutes. Add all the mussels and the parsley into the sauce. Heat 1 minute more.

Drain the pasta and transfer it to individual serving dishes. Ladle sauce over the pasta. Decorate each plate with the unshelled mussels. Sprinkle with grated cheese and, if your taste lies in that direction, some crushed red pepper.

Serves 2–3.

Polpette

THERE IS A CURIOUS story among Italians which says that Sicilians cannot make anything round, including meatballs. The insinuation is that we lack the sophistication and necessary skills required.

It is true that Sicilian meatballs *(polpette)* are not round like a ball. They have a flattened oval shape, much like a stepped-on football. It is, perhaps, this shape that has given rise to the further vile canard that Sicilians make meatballs with their feet.

This lie is similar to the cruel and baseless tale that only northern Italians write cookbooks because literacy ends somewhere south of Naples. To refute this, I shall undertake, at any given time, to assemble as many as six authentic Sicilians capable of signing their full names!

But regarding polpette, I wish to deal with another rumor, which claims that we clumsily keep dropping the meat on the floor, where it is then trampled upon by the goat. May I point out that, were this so, the print of the goat's hoof would be discernible.

And yet, this story and others like them abound among our northern compatriots. We deserve better treatment, especially from our neighbors, whom we have neither harmed nor taken advantage of—unless it was absolutely necessary, or profitable.

Pasta with Meatballs

Pasta con Polpette di Carne

You will need:

For 4-6 servings (about 1½ lbs) of pasta and 1½ dozen polpette

1 cup	Seasoned Bread Crumbs (see page 59)		2	cloves garlic, minced
1 quart	Marinara Sauce (see page 102)		½ cup	fresh, chopped parsley
1 lb	ground beef		1 tbsp	oregano
½ lb	ground pork		1 tbsp	dried basil
1	small white onion, minced			salt and pepper to taste
			3	eggs, beaten
				extra virgin olive oil

Preparation:

Prepare bread crumbs and marinara sauce, and begin heating the sauce.

Combine beef and pork in a large bowl, mixing well. Add the onion, garlic, parsley, bread crumbs, oregano, basil, and salt and pepper, making sure all ingredients are well distributed. Blend in the eggs so the mixture is moist.

Spoon some of the mixture into the palm of your hand (keeping in mind you'll be making 1½ dozen polpette) and form the polpette by cupping both palms together. The result will be an oval shape instead of the traditional round meatball. (The reason for this odd shape will be obvious as soon as you brown the meatballs in a skillet: you need brown only two sides, thereby preventing the polpette from overcooking and becoming tough or rubbery.)

Heat a little olive oil in a skillet and fast fry the polpette over moderately high heat, being careful not to overcook them. As soon as they brown, transfer to the bubbling sauce. Then allow the polpette to finish cooking in the simmering sauce for at least half an hour.

Serves 4–6.

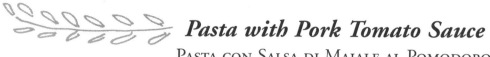 

Pasta with Pork Tomato Sauce
PASTA CON SALSA DI MAIALE AL POMODORO

The following recipe can be used with pork of any kind, though most often a cheap package of neck bones serves best. In this case, pork spare ribs (country style) are used. It doesn't matter whether they are deboned or not. You should be warned that this is one of those dark, rich sauces that will take more than an hour of simmering time to do it justice. Also, your choice of pasta is up to you as this goes with linguine as easily as with mostacciole.

You will need:

For 4–6 servings
of pasta (about 1 ½ lbs)

1 ½ lbs	country style spare ribs (trim off all excess fat)		1 can	(28 oz) whole tomatoes, broken up
½ cup	extra virgin olive oil		½ cup	fresh, chopped basil leaves
1 tsp	fennel seeds		½ cup	sweet red wine
6	cloves of garlic, finely chopped		1 tbsp	sugar
1	medium onion, coarsely chopped		salt and pepper to taste	
2 tbsp	dried oregano		¼ cup	fresh, chopped parsley
1 can	(28 oz) crushed tomatoes			

Preparation:

Heat 1 tablespoon of olive oil in a large saucepan over medium heat. Add the fennel seeds and then the spare ribs. Brown the ribs on all sides, then remove from pan and set aside. Add the rest of the olive oil to the pan and, when hot, stir in the garlic, onion, and oregano.

Pour in both the crushed and the broken-up tomatoes when the onions turn translucent, then add the basil. Bring sauce to a bubble and then add the wine. Continue cooking on high heat for another 5 minutes. Add sugar to sauce and then the salt and pepper. Return the ribs to the pan. Adjust heat so that the sauce will simmer while covered.

Simmer for at least an hour, checking every 15 minutes or so to be sure the sauce doesn't begin to burn. Add wine or hot water if the sauce gets too thick. Check for taste and tenderness. The meat on the ribs must be tender and about to fall off the bone. Just before the pasta is ready, remove the ribs from the sauce and set aside. Pour the sauce over the hot pasta and then place the ribs on top. Sprinkle minced parsley over the dish and serve.

Serves 4-6.

IN THIS COUNTRY, it is usual to take some things for granted. We even have people who eat meat as often as three times in the same day. In the old country, however, meat was something of a luxury, and still is for that matter. Well, this is their bad luck for the time being. I do not wish to sound unsympathetic, but I am here now, and things go very well for me and my family. You must have noticed how an abundance of good food makes people optimistic and cheerful. There is really very little to worry about if we have our health and a full belly.

For Sicilians, seafood (since there is more of it) is more important than poultry, beef, or lamb. And though they use pork in sausage and salami, Sicilians are not overly fond of it. Probably this is the result of the Arab in us, though it may be due to expense as much as inclination.

Long ago, we had some beautiful neighbors who made a pasta sauce every evening, and it always was made by adding a few neck bones of beef or pork or even veal. At supper, the bones were piled mid-table and the children would joyously gnaw anything softer than their teeth. I recall the parents' happy contentment at having meat on their table every day. They took it upon their salvation that living in this country was a step up on anyone's social ladder. I should add that these people were Barese, which might explain this phenomenon.

Well, enough of such pleasantries. We must move on to the vegetables.

Pasta with Vegetables

I T WILL BE OBVIOUS to the experienced eater that nearly any kind of vegetable can be mixed with pasta to the benefit of both. What you should consider is the taste you seek, and then create a sauce most appropriate to the vegetable you are using. For example, pasta with beans has a full-flavored, heavy taste. Pasta with artichokes has a subtle, delicate flavor. And pasta with peas lies somewhere between the two.

Many vegetable-pasta dishes are put together by using a marinara sauce and then adding a vegetable—zucchini and mushrooms are good examples —as it cooks. There is no real reason to set down a separate recipe for these types of sauces. Just remember that zucchini take longer to cook than mushrooms, so add them at the beginning rather than at the end. Remember also that zucchini will break apart if overcooked. Mushrooms, as they cook, throw out water, shrinking and becoming rubbery; so allow them no more than 5 minutes in the pot.

Pasta with Artichokes
PASTA CON CARCIOFI

You will need:

For 2–3 servings of pasta
(mostaccioli is good)

3	slices bacon, cut small	1 pkg	(10 oz) frozen
4 tbsp	extra virgin olive oil		artichoke hearts
1	medium onion, minced	salt and pepper to taste	
1 can	(28 oz) crushed plum tomatoes	handful fresh, chopped parsley	
3–4	fresh, chopped basil leaves	grated Romano cheese	
4 tbsp	dry white wine		

Preparation:

   Cook the bacon in a medium saucepan until brown, then drain off the fat. Add olive oil and combine the onion with the bacon, sautéing until the onion turns translucent. Add tomatoes and basil and bring to a simmer. Add wine and cook at high heat for 5 minutes. Cover and simmer 10 minutes.

   Add the artichokes and return to a simmer. Add the salt and pepper and stir gently from time to time. Remove pan from heat when artichokes are tender, then pour the mixture over the pasta. Sprinkle with fresh parsley and grated cheese.

Serves 2–3.

Pasta and Beans
Pasta e Fagioli

Various types of beans will do, though cannellini (white kidney beans) are best.

You will need:

For 3–4 servings of pasta (small shell or elbow macaroni is good), about 1 lb

4 tbsp	extra virgin olive oil	1	tbsp oregano
3	cloves garlic, minced	1	can of cannellini or similar
1	medium onion, chopped		beans, drained
1 cup	Chicken Broth (see page 66)		grated Romano cheese
salt and pepper to taste			

Preparation:

Heat olive oil in a saucepan, then sauté the garlic and onion until the onion turns translucent. Add the chicken broth, salt, pepper, and oregano. Simmer for 10 minutes.

Add the beans and bring back to a simmer. When the beans are warmed through, pour the mixture over the pasta and toss well. Allow to stand for 5 minutes so pasta can absorb the flavors. Sprinkle with grated cheese and serve.

Serves 3–4.

Variation: For Pasta and Beans with Broccoli/*Pasta e Fagioli con Broccoli*, follow the same recipe, but add a package of frozen broccoli heads after the beans. Simmer the sauce, covered, until the broccoli is tender (about 10 minutes). Cook the pasta till al dente, then add it to the sauce. Simmer together for 5 minutes.

Pasta with Eggplant

PASTA CON MELANZANE

The following are a few of many ways of combining pasta with eggplant. Just remember that the best of Italian cooking is like the best of American jazz music: a combination of improvisation, experience, and luck.

You will need:

For 4–6 servings of pasta (about 1 ½ lbs)

1 cup	extra virgin olive oil (more as needed)	2 lbs	plum tomatoes, peeled and chopped (or one 28 oz can crushed tomatoes)
3	large eggplants, sliced, salted, and drained at least an hour (see instructions on page 38)	6–8	fresh, chopped basil leaves
			salt and pepper to taste
5–6	cloves garlic, sliced		grated Romano cheese

Preparation:

Heat olive oil in a large skillet. Brown the eggplant slices in batches, starting with ¼ cup of oil and adding more as needed. Transfer the eggplant to paper towels when tender. Don't discard any remaining oil, but sauté the garlic in it and then add the tomatoes. Bring to a boil, lower to a simmer, and add the basil and salt and pepper. Simmer 20 minutes and then remove from heat.

When the pasta is ready, pour the tomato mixture over it. Then place the eggplant slices on top and sprinkle with grated cheese.

Serves 4–6.

Variation: Simmer the sauce for only 10 minutes and then mix half the sauce into the pasta. Brush a large baking dish with olive oil, then line it with half the fried eggplant. Arrange a layer of pasta over the eggplant, then sprinkle chopped basil and grated cheese on top. Layer the remaining eggplant, the pasta, and the sauce. Sprinkle grated Romano cheese on top and then bake 10–15 minutes in a hot (450°) oven.

More variations: It should come as no surprise to learn that Sicilians will put nearly anything into these eggplant dishes, including chunks of mozzarella cheese, bits of salami, chopped black olives, capers, and, naturally, the ubiquitous anchovy. If any of these appeal to you, do not hesitate.

Pasta Primavera

Pasta Primavera (springtime) is a fine Sicilian invention which strives to bring the very freshest taste of vegetables to the dish. Indeed, the only recipe I know of that tastes fresher uses uncooked "oil and vinegar salad" to mix with hot pasta. It is not only fresher, it is completely raw.

Since this sauce cooks very quickly, perhaps 10 minutes at the most, it is best to have all the vegetables ready and cut before you begin. In fact, it is best to start cooking the pasta before the sauce.

You will need:

For 3–4 servings of pasta (rigatoni and penne work well), about 1 lb

4 tbsp	butter		1	zucchini, sliced
4 tbsp	extra virgin olive oil		3–4	green onions, sliced
¼ cup	slivered prosciutto (can substitute ham)		1 pkg	(10 oz) frozen tiny peas
½ lb	asparagus tips and chopped stems		5–6	fresh, chopped basil leaves
½ lb	sliced mushrooms			salt and pepper to taste
1	carrot, thinly sliced (use a potato peeler)			handful fresh, chopped parsley
				grated Romano cheese

Preparation:

Heat the butter and olive oil in a saucepan before adding prosciutto, asparagus, mushrooms, carrot, and zucchini. Stir, cover, and cook over moderate heat for 5 minutes.

Add the green onions, peas, basil, and salt and pepper. Increase heat until the mixture starts to boil, then reduce to a simmer and continue cooking, covered, another 4–5 minutes.

Pour the mixture over hot pasta and mix gently. Sprinkle with parsley and grated cheese.

Serves 3–4.

Pasta with Peas
PASTA CON PISELLI

You will need:

**For 3–4 servings of small
shell pasta (about 1 lb)**

4 tbsp	extra virgin olive oil
2	cloves garlic, minced
1	medium onion, finely chopped
1 pkg	(10 oz) frozen peas
2 tbsp	oregano

2 cups   Chicken Broth (see page 66)

salt and pepper to taste

handful fresh, chopped parsley

grated Romano cheese

Preparation:

Heat olive oil in a saucepan, then sauté the garlic and onion until the onion turns translucent. Add the frozen peas, turning them in the pan until thawed and separated. Add the oregano, chicken broth, and salt and pepper. Bring to a boil before lowering heat and simmering for 15 minutes.

Cook the pasta until al dente. Mix the drained pasta into the pot of sauce and heat for 3–5 minutes. Transfer pasta and sauce mixture into a serving bowl and sprinkle with parsley and grated cheese.

Serves 3–4.

Pasta with Cauliflower
PASTA CON CAVOLFIORE

You may have noticed that I like to win arguments and that I will, at times, go to great lengths to prove my point of view. This is a natural failing on my part and one that I find completely forgivable. It is with this in mind that I offer a pair of recipes which demonstrate my view that Sicilians will mix nearly anything with pasta. You will scarcely believe it.

You will need:

For 3-4 servings of pasta (rigatoni and penne work well), about 1 lb

½ cup	extra virgin olive oil		1	medium cauliflower, divided into florets
2	cloves garlic, minced			
2 lbs	plum tomatoes, peeled and chopped (or one 28 oz can crushed tomatoes)		1 cup	Chicken Broth (see page 66)

salt and pepper to taste

grated Romano cheese

Preparation:

Heat olive oil in a saucepan, then sauté the garlic until just golden. Add the tomatoes, crushing them with a fork as they cook. Bring to a gentle boil and add the cauliflower, broth, and salt and pepper. Cover and cook for about 30–40 minutes over low heat. The sauce will thicken as the cauliflower breaks up.

Pour the sauce over hot pasta and sprinkle with grated cheese.

Serves 3-4.

Pasta with Cabbage

PASTA CON CAVOLO

You will need:

For 3-4 servings of pasta (rigatoni and penne are good choices), about 1 lb

4 tbsp	extra virgin olive oil	salt and pepper to taste
1	medium onion, chopped	grated Romano cheese
1	head cabbage, cored and chopped bite-size	

Preparation:

Heat olive oil in a saucepan and sauté the onion until translucent. Add the cabbage and salt and pepper. Cover and steam for about 30 minutes.

Cook the pasta until al dente. Do not drain completely, but leave about 1 cup of the water in the pot with the pasta.

Add the cabbage to the pasta. Allow to stand 2–3 minutes before serving with grated cheese.

Serves 3–4.

Seafood

PESCE

ICILIANS, SURROUNDED BY the sea, are naturally intrigued by any chance of food to be had in that direction. They take any shellfish or any fish, from the smallest eel or anchovy to a large tuna or even a swordfish that swims by.

In this country it has been a little more difficult—especially since the early days of World War II, when New York Harbor was dredged to allow the big warships in. The resultant silt drove out all the tommy-cod and flounder. I recall the tragic day when every fisherman on the East River toiled in vain.

We, too, had, as the saying goes, "fished all night and caught nothing." Rather than return empty-handed, we scavenged the rocks and pilings and took over 20 pounds of periwinkles. These we boiled with lemon, vinegar, and salt and heaped in a huge mound on the table, attacking them with pins and laughter. There is probably a lesson to be learned here, but at the moment I feel too sluggish to pursue it.

After the last chapter, one would think all sauce possibilities had been exhausted. One would be wrong. Now come, do not take this badly. It is no disgrace to find fewer limitations in food, fine ideas, or the flight of birds than one might have previously imagined. It is rather heartening.

Let us speak of some sauces. The first three are recipes for baking fish with wine. In one, a sweet vermouth is used and in the other two, a dry wine with spices. In each, the sauce may be poured over the fish as it bakes or used to baste the baking fish. A word of warning: fish throw out water as they bake, so a small amount of sauce goes a long way.

Then there is a white cream sauce that may be used for fish, though in truth it is more usually found with chicken or vegetables. I add it here to demonstrate my "international" flair. Finally, there is a spiced sauce that can be used either hot or cold with fish.

There is really nothing magical about sauces, no matter what the French believe, and I group them together here so that you will at once see their similarities. This will get your mind working, and you might strike out with enterprises and inclinations of your own. And why not? No one who has journeyed so far in this book will ever be considered a coward.

Wine Sauce for Baked Fish #1

Salsa al Vino per Pesce al Forno #1

Here are three versions of this dish. We assume you will be baking a thick white fish, such as halibut, sea bass, or swordfish. Your oven will be preheated to a moderate 350–375°, and you will start to check for flaking after 15 minutes of total baking time. (Time depends upon the thickness of the fish.)

With tarragon and vermouth

You will need:

3 tbsp	extra virgin olive oil		salt and pepper to taste
I	small onion, minced	1 cup	Chicken Broth (see page 66)
½ tsp	tarragon	4 tbsp	sweet (white) vermouth

Preparation:

Preheat oven (see above), and begin baking the fish when the sauce is nearly done.

Heat olive oil, then sauté the onion, along with the tarragon and salt and pepper, until it is translucent. Add the broth. Cook over medium heat for 15 minutes, then add the vermouth and cook an additional 15 minutes.

Pour the sauce over the fish after it has been baking for 10 minutes and continue baking until the flesh is flaky, checking after about 5 minutes.

Yields 1½ cups.

Wine Sauce for Baked Fish #2

Salsa al Vino per Pesce al Forno #2

With cloves and white wine

You will need:

3 tbsp	extra virgin olive oil		salt and pepper to taste
I	small onion, minced	1 cup	Chicken Broth (see page 66)
I tsp	thyme	⅓ cup	dry white wine
I tsp	oregano	I tsp	lemon juice
¼ tsp	ground cloves	I tsp	sugar

Preparation:

Preheat oven to 350–375°, and begin baking the fish when the sauce is nearly done.

Heat olive oil, then sauté the onion, along with the thyme, oregano, cloves, and salt and pepper, until it is translucent. Add the broth. Cook over medium heat for 15 minutes, then add the wine, lemon juice, and sugar. Cook an additional 15 minutes.

Pour the sauce over the fish after it has been baking for 10 minutes and continue baking until the flesh is flaky, checking after about 5 minutes.

Yields 1½ cups.

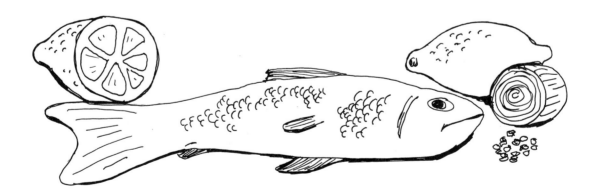

 **_Wine Sauce for Baked Fish #3_**
SALSA AL VINO PER PESCE AL FORNO #3

***With oregano, tarragon,
and white wine***

You will need:

4 tbsp	extra virgin olive oil	I cup	dry white wine
I	small onion, minced	salt and pepper to taste	
2–3	cloves garlic, sliced	juice of I lemon	
½ tsp	oregano		
½ tsp	tarragon		

Preparation:

Heat olive oil in a large pan or skillet, then sauté the garlic and onion until the onion turns translucent, about 4–5 minutes. Along the way add the oregano and tarragon.

Add the wine, then bring to a boil and continue to cook on high heat until the liquid is reduced by half. Add the salt and pepper. Remove from heat, then stir in the lemon juice.

Allow the mixture to cool. It is now ready to baste any fish you are baking or grilling.

Yields 1½ cups.

White Cream Sauce
SALSA ALLA BESCIAMELLA

You will need:

4 tbsp	melted butter	¼ tsp	tarragon
4 tbsp	all-purpose flour		white pepper to taste
2 cups	half-and-half cream		salt to taste
2	bay leaves		

Preparation:

Melt the butter over low heat in a small frying pan, then whisk in the flour until smooth. Add the half-and-half and whisk briskly into a thick cream. Cook over medium heat and add the remaining ingredients, stirring to avoid lumps. Remove from heat when the mixture has thickened, and discard the bay leaves.

Yields 2½ cups.

Note: This sauce can be used not only with fish, but also with vegetables and poultry. If using with steamed vegetables, drain their juices to avoid diluting the sauce.

ONE OF THE THINGS New York offers is tiny shops that specialize in shellfish. They are found only in Italian areas and feature little wooden tables and chairs, so the customer can eat on the spot. They have cherrystone clams, oysters, mussels, and larger crustaceans lying on piles of chipped ice. In the middle of shopping, you can stop and order a dozen or so, on the half shell and served with fresh lemon and various sauces. You can sit with your shopping bags about you and wait for the owner to bring you the first dozen. No matter what troubles you might have, you somehow know that God has not abandoned the human race.

Spicy Sauce for Seafood
SALSA PICCANTE PER PESCE DI MARE

This makes a good sauce for baking stuffed squid. However, it is also useful to serve chilled for shellfish or as a dip with antipasto. It will keep several weeks in the refrigerator.

You will need:

4 tbsp	extra virgin olive oil	1 tbsp	sugar
1	small onion, minced	3 tbsp	grated horseradish (coarse)
1 tsp	oregano	1 tbsp	Tabasco sauce
salt and pepper to taste		juice of 1 lemon	
1 can	(28 oz) crushed plum tomatoes	1 tsp	sugar (optional)
¼ tsp	garlic salt		

Preparation:

Heat olive oil in a large skillet, then sauté the onion for 5 minutes, sprinkling in the oregano and salt and pepper. Add the tomatoes. Simmer for 10 minutes, then add the garlic salt and the sugar. Simmer another 20 minutes, stir, and set aside.

Add horseradish when the mixture is cool, along with the Tabasco sauce and lemon juice. The sauce should have a semi-sweet, nippy flavor with a good, refreshing aftertaste. If too tart, add a teaspoon of sugar.

Yields 4 cups.

Note: A simpler version uses ketchup, horseradish, lemon juice, Tabasco sauce, and a little sugar and onion salt. It is not Sicilian, but that never bothered us before—so why should you mind.

Baccalà

BACCALÀ IS A FISH favored throughout Italy. It is nearly always cooked or baked with tomatoes, though some add cabbage and some sweet red peppers. In Bologna they season it with cloves and in Florence with rosemary. Everyone has their own style in approaching this lovely dish. Sicilians are prone to throw in pine nuts and raisins, with a lot of fennel for taste. I never approved of such extravagance.

Obviously popular and great holiday fare, what is surprising is that it was probably introduced (via Sicily, of course) by invading Vikings about a thousand or so years ago. It is unusual for Sicilians to pick up northern European eating habits, but who can argue with history?

Anyone who has been in an Italian market has seen baccalà stacked, strange looking and gray, in boxes and barrels and even hanging from the ceiling. A most unappetizing sight. In recent times, the fish is salt-dried; but years ago, when salt was as expensive as caviar, it was usual to simply dry it in the sun, and it was known as stockfish.

By the way, modern shopping places can still be a joy. Many markets, you know, have baskets of marked-down cans that have lost their labels. It is always worthwhile to buy a few and spend some time at home guessing as to the contents before opening them. A word of advice: always shake the can. If it is so tightly packed that nothing rattles or slushes about inside, it is probably dog food, and I recommend you reject it.

Baccalà

Salt Cod alla Siciliana

It is necessary that you prepare the baccalà first. This means washing and placing the fish (after cutting it into 2″ squares) into cold water to soak. To remove the salt, you have to keep the fish refrigerated in water from 24 to 48 hours, changing the water every 8 hours. Finally, drain and dry the fish, and remove the skin, bones, and cartilage. Now you are ready.

You will need:

2 lbs	dried salt cod, prepared (see above)
½ cup	extra virgin olive oil
2	onions, diced
3–4	cloves garlic, sliced
pepper to taste	
chili powder (to taste)	
1 tsp	tarragon
2 lbs	plum tomatoes, peeled and chopped (or one 28 oz can crushed tomatoes)
½ cup	dry white wine (plus additional, if needed)
1 cup	chopped celery
1 lb	potatoes, cut into bite-size chunks (about 2 cups)
2 tbsp	capers
handful pitted green olives	
juice of 1 lemon	
handful fresh, chopped parsley	

Preparation:

Heat ¼ cup of the olive oil in a saucepan, and sauté 1 onion and the garlic until the onion turns translucent. Add pepper, chili powder, and tarragon and simmer 5 minutes. Add tomatoes and raise heat to bubbling. Cook at medium heat for 10 minutes, add the wine, and cook at medium-high heat for another 10 minutes.

Preheat oven to 375°. Heat the remaining ¼ cup of olive oil in an attractive ovenproof pan, along with the second onion and the celery. Simmer 10 minutes, then mix in the potatoes and cook, covered, for 15 minutes. Stir several times to keep the potatoes from sticking.

Add the fish to the ovenproof pan, then add the tomato mixture. Mix gently while adding the capers and olives. Bake, covered, 30–40 minutes, mixing carefully from time to time while tasting for salt. Add wine if the sauce gets too thick. The fish will flake when done. Make sure the potatoes are tender.

Serve from the pan. Squeeze lemon juice over the fish and garnish with parsley. You will be pleasantly surprised at how mild and soothing this formidable dish will taste.

Serves 6–8.

Marinated Eel
ANGUILLA MARINATA

Eel is a wonderful animal. It can be fried with herbs and served hot or cold. It can be cooked in wine sauce, or it can be added, just like fried sausage, to tomato sauce for pasta. And it is very good, too. Naturally, you will have to clean it first and prepare it for the pot.

To clean the eel you proceed much as you would with catfish. (Catfish are best cleaned after driving a nail through a board and impaling the fish's head on the nail.) First, slit the belly and remove the contents. Then slice a collar around the neck, just below the head, and work a bit of skin loose to peel downwards. A pair of pliers helps here, and the skin will peel down to the tail. The dorsal fins and head can then be easily removed.

Wash and pat the eel dry, rub with lemon, and cut into 3″ pieces. Now you are ready.

This dish needs to marinate for at least 24 hours.

You will need:

For the marinade

1 cup	Fish Broth (see page 68)
½ cup	extra virgin olive oil
2	large onions, sliced
4–5	cloves garlic, minced
2	bay leaves, crumbled
½ tsp	oregano
½ tsp	thyme
3–4	whole cloves

5–6	whole peppercorns
1 tbsp	salt
1 cup	white wine vinegar

For the eel

2–3 lbs	eel (3″ pieces)
1	lemon, cut in half
	all-purpose flour (for rolling the eel)

Preparation:

Prepare the marinade. Heat half the olive oil and sauté the onions for 4–5 minutes. Add the bay leaves, oregano, thyme, cloves, peppercorns, and salt. Stir and simmer 5 minutes. Add fish broth and vinegar. Simmer 15–20 minutes, uncovered. Keep hot.

Prepare the eel. Rub the pieces with lemon and roll them in flour. Heat the remaining olive oil in a separate pan and brown the eel. Turn to brown on all sides, but do not overcook.

Place the browned eel in a large glass or ceramic dish. Pour the hot marinade over the eel until the container is filled to the brim. Cover tightly with a lid, plastic wrap, or foil, and refrigerate at least a full day. You will find the eel has thrown out a gelatin that has thickened the whole affair.

Serves 8–10.

MANY PEOPLE HAVE never tasted eel, and this is their sore loss. In some eastern rivers, they are very nearly the only thing left to catch, so unhappily have we dealt with our waterways.

I recall seeing a terrible thing while fishing under the great bridge that spans to New Jersey. Someone had caught a capitan—the huge conger eel three feet long that gives so many wonderful steaks—and had left it to decay on the rocks. What a sad and shameful thing to do. The fool might at least have thrown it back if he did not wish to keep it. So many years ago this was, and still I taste the anger at the sight. Enough.

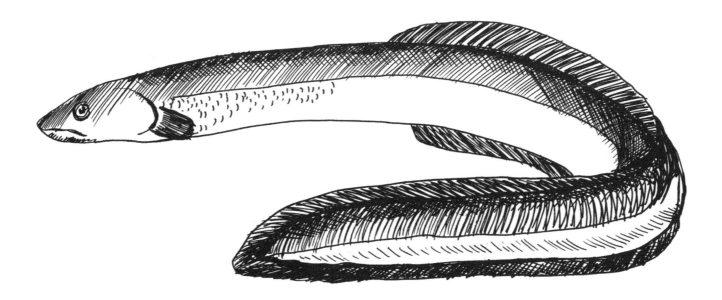

Stewed Fish
Zuppa di Pesce

Stewed fish is not fish stew. This dish is warmly regarded by all Italians, who call it zuppa. But zuppa doesn't really mean "soup," even if it sounds like it does. It means "to soften by immersing." Perhaps the term that should be used for stew is *stracotto*, or perhaps *stufato.*

I suggest you choose at least three different types of fish to start. Haddock, flounder, cod, perch, bass, and snapper—anything that is firm-fleshed and lacks oil—are all good choices. Avoid mackerel, tuna, and the like. Cut the fish into 2″ serving pieces. Here is what you do:

You will need:

6 lbs	whole fish (2 lbs each of 3 types of fish)	½ tsp	cayenne pepper
			salt and pepper to taste
½ lb	shrimp (shells on)		pinch saffron (optional)
½ lb	squid, chopped	½ cup	extra virgin olive oil
1 lb	mussels, cleaned and bearded	1 cup	dry white wine
1	onion, sliced		several slices Italian bread
2–3	cloves garlic, minced		olive oil (for browning the bread)
12	black olives, pitted		peel of 1 lemon, grated
6	peppercorns		handful fresh, chopped parsley

Preparation:

Preheat oven to 350°.

Use a large casserole dish with tight-fitting cover. Arrange in layers: the fish on the bottom, then the shrimp, then the squid, and finally the mussels on top. Sprinkle first with onion, garlic, olives, peppercorns, cayenne pepper, salt and pepper, and saffron (if used). Then sprinkle with olive oil and wine.

Place the casserole in the oven and bake, covered, for 30–35 minutes. Discard any mussels that have not opened.

Ladle the stew over thick slices of Italian bread that have been browned in olive oil. Add grated lemon peel and chopped parsley over individual servings.

The saffron is optional because it is so expensive.

Serves 8–10.

Red Mullet
TRIGLIE

You will need:

6	small red mullet, scaled and cleaned	4 tbsp	Chicken or Fish Broth (see pages 66 and 68)
4 tbsp	extra virgin olive oil	4 tbsp	dry white wine
	salt and pepper to taste		juice of 1 lemon and 1 orange
	grated peel of 1 lemon and 1 orange	4 tbsp	butter
			hot pepper sauce (optional)

Preparation:

Marinate the fish for an hour in olive oil, salt, and pepper.

Prepare the sauce. Combine the grated lemon and orange peels with the broth and wine in a saucepan, then bring to a boil. Remove from heat and add the citrus juices and butter. (You may want to consider a dash of hot pepper sauce to enliven the taste.) Keep hot.

Grill or broil the fish—3″ or so from the element—about 3 minutes per side.

Serve hot, with the sauce poured over the fish.

Serves 3–4.

Now HERE IS A FISH with a history as old as the Pekingese dog of China. Mullet run in huge schools, and Italians have been netting them for several thousand years. In this country, the mullet is found mainly on the east coast and is a commercial fish—some fifty or sixty thousand pounds per season being caught. On the west coast, the striped mullet can grow to several feet, but the eastern and the Mediterranean varieties are much smaller. You will scarcely believe this, but Sicilians grill them whole, the insides being regarded as a delicacy. I would not bother recommending this to you, since not everyone has such fortitude; but I mention it as a curiosity so that you will stand amazed at your close escape by being lucky enough to have been born elsewhere when mullet was first eaten.

It is an ugly fish, too.

Stuffed Baked Sardines
SARDE RIPIENE AL FORNO

Fresh sardines, unlike their canned relatives, are 6–8″ long and somewhat difficult to find … outside of bait shops.

You will need:

3 lbs	fresh sardines		handful fresh, chopped parsley
½ cup	extra virgin olive oil (plus additional for drizzling)	½ cup	pine nuts
		½ cup	raisins
1 cup	bread crumbs	1 can	anchovies, drained and chopped fine
2 tbsp	capers		
2–3	cloves garlic, sliced	2–3	crumbled bay leaves
½ cup	pitted black olives, sliced		juice of 1 lemon

Preparation:

Clean the fish and remove head and fins. Split in half and remove backbone. Wash in salt water and dry on paper towels. Set aside.

Heat ¼ cup of the olive oil, then add all but a handful of the bread crumbs and stir until they begin to brown. Add the capers, garlic, olives, parsley, pine nuts, raisins, and anchovies. Mix well. Stir fry 5 minutes and remove from heat.

Preheat oven to 375°. Spread some of the mixture on each sardine. Roll the sardines up from neck to tail, and fasten with toothpicks so that tails stick up in the air. Spread the remaining ¼ cup of olive oil in the bottom of a baking dish. Place the sardines in rows—*do not piggy-back.* Sprinkle bits of bay leaves, the remaining handful of dry bread crumbs, and a bit of olive oil over the fish and bake 25–30 minutes.

Serve with a little lemon juice squeezed on top.

Serves 4–6.

Fillet of Sole
Filetti di Sogliole

These go well served over fresh rice or other grains.

You will need:

2 tbsp	extra virgin olive oil	I tbsp	chopped basil leaves
I	medium onion, coarsely chopped	I	large, ripe tomato, peeled
3	cloves garlic, minced		and chopped
salt and pepper to taste		I tsp	sugar
I tbsp	fresh, chopped parsley	I lb	fillet of sole
		juice of ½ lemon	

Preparation:

Heat olive oil in a large, covered skillet, then sauté onion and garlic until the onion is translucent. Add the salt and pepper, parsley, and basil leaves and stir, simmering, for another minute. Add the tomato and stir gently. Cook for about 10 minutes. Taste for tartness, and add sugar if necessary.

Arrange the fillets flat in the skillet, then spread the mixture over them. Add lemon juice and cover. Cook for about 10 minutes at medium heat, testing for flaking. Remove from heat when done.

Serve hot over steamed rice—or whatever other good thing comes to mind.

Serves 3–4.

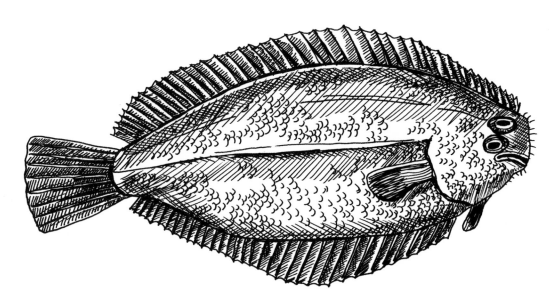

Baked Fillet of Sole in Wine Sauce
FILETTI DI SOGLIOLE AL FORNO AL VINO BIANCO

You will need:

2 lbs	sole, washed and patted dry
flour (for dredging)	
3 tbsp	butter
1	small onion, finely chopped
3	cloves garlic, minced
1 tsp	oregano
2	canned anchovies, drained

handful fresh, chopped parsley	
1 tbsp	capers
½ cup	dry white wine
salt and pepper to taste	
juice of 1 lemon	

Preparation:

Flour the fillets and set them aside. Heat the butter in a skillet, then add the onion, garlic, oregano, and anchovies. Mash the anchovies, stir, and simmer until the onion starts to brown. Add the parsley, capers, wine, and salt and pepper. Simmer 10 minutes, then remove from heat.

Preheat oven to 375°. Place a layer of fish in a shallow casserole dish with cover. Spoon some of the anchovy sauce over the fish. Continue layering, finishing up with a layer of sauce.

Cover the casserole, then set it on the middle rack and bake 30 minutes. Test the fish to make sure it flakes. Remove from oven and set aside for 5 minutes.

Serve sprinkled with lemon juice.

Serves 4–6

Baked Swordfish
Pescespada al Forno

You will need:

2	swordfish steaks, 1–1 ½ lbs each	handful fresh, chopped basil leaves
½ cup	extra virgin olive oil	salt and pepper to taste
2–3	cloves garlic, sliced	4 tbsp dry white wine
2 lbs	plum tomatoes, peeled and chopped	juice of 1 lemon
		handful fresh, chopped parsley

Preparation:

Preheat oven to 400°.

Heat olive oil, sauté the garlic, and add the tomatoes just before the garlic browns. Break up the tomatoes with a fork, then add the basil and stir in salt and pepper. Simmer for 15 minutes. Add the wine, raise heat till the liquid boils, and stir. Continue to cook on high heat for about 5 minutes. Keep the sauce hot.

Arrange the swordfish steaks in a well-oiled baking dish, then pour the sauce on top. Sprinkle with lemon juice and bake, uncovered, for 20 minutes or until the fish starts to flake.

Serve sprinkled with parsley.

Serves 2–4.

Variation: Sicilians have a nice, simple way to fry swordfish, which could probably apply to any large fish from which steaks are taken. Thin swordfish steaks are rubbed with lemon and then dredged in flour. Salt and pepper are sprinkled over the top, and the fish are fried at medium heat in olive oil. When done, they are served with capers and fresh parsley sprinkled on top—and an extra squeeze of lemon for luck.

Brother Devil's Lobster
Aragosta Fra Diavolo

You will need:

2	medium lobsters, cooked	1 tsp	oregano
½ cup	extra virgin olive oil	salt and pepper to taste	
1	small onion, diced	1 cup	dry white wine
2	cloves garlic, minced	½ tsp	crushed red pepper
1 ½ lbs	plum tomatoes, peeled and chopped	1 tbsp	grated Romano cheese
		handful fresh, chopped parsley	

Preparation:

Clean the lobsters and remove the small claws. Empty stomach cavities and discard lungs and veins. Crack the large claws.

Heat olive oil in a large frying pan, then add the lobsters—including the claws—and cook over low heat, covered, for 5 minutes. Remove lobsters from heat, keeping them warm while you prepare the sauce.

Sauté the onion and garlic in the same pan for 5 minutes. Add the tomatoes, oregano, and salt and pepper. Simmer 15 minutes. Add the wine, raise heat so the sauce starts to bubble, and cook on medium-high heat for another 5 minutes.

Add the crushed red pepper along with the cheese, parsley, and lobsters. Baste the lobsters well, cover the pan, and simmer for 5 minutes.

Serves 2.

The Adaptable Squid

THERE WAS A TIME when the lowest prices at the meat and seafood market were found in the fish section, and scallops and crab cost a fraction of the price of beef. That was history, which, as you know, never improves with age. So far, the clever squid has escaped the fate of its more popular cousins, perhaps the result of its appearance. Yet its meat is as fine as the most expensive shellfish, and its versatility is surpassed only by the chicken. Squid can be stewed or stuffed, fried or baked. It can complement other dishes (fish or fowl) or stand its ground as a main course. And it makes a beautiful sauce.

Squid can be bought fresh or frozen. If frozen, I recommend that after cleaning it, you leave the squid soaking in salt water—squeeze in some lemon juice—for a few hours. This will resolve any miscalculations regarding its age.

It is possible that many people stand baffled at its color and intricacy and shrink from attacking for fear of failure. Attend! The color comes off by merely rubbing the skin, and the intricacy is addressed with a sharp knife. With a gentle tug, a squid will separate into two parts. The hood or mantle is cleaned by emptying its contents, peeling the skin (rub it under running water), and tearing off the fins. The lower part is even easier. Hold the tentacles on a counter and slice it in half directly below the eyes. Then hold the tentacles upside-down and pluck out the beak or quill.

Thus, the thing is done. A child could learn it in a few minutes.

At this point, you are able to slice the hood so that it forms rings. These can be deep-fried in olive oil or breaded like shrimp. The tentacles can be handled in the same manner.

The shape of the hood is, of course, an invitation for stuffing. There is no particularly classic formula for stuffing. See what your pantry or refrigerator holds, and be brave. Bread crumbs with various seasonings are good, but if you have some old cheese or salami you were about to throw away, invest them with the dignity of service and make a meal of them. A raw egg will bind and hide many incongruities.

I remind you only that squid cooks rapidly and then starts getting tough.

Baked Stuffed Squid
Calamari Ripieni al Forno

You will need:

12	squid	handful fresh, chopped basil leaves
1 recipe for Stuffing for Squid		4 tbsp dry red wine
	(see opposite page)	salt and pepper to taste
4 tbsp	extra virgin olive oil	handful fresh, chopped parsley
3	cloves garlic, sliced	(for garnish)
1 can	(28 oz) plum tomatoes, crushed	lemon wedges (for garnish)

Preparation:

Clean the squid by following the instructions on page 155. Chop up the fins and the tentacles, which you will add to the stuffing.

Prepare the stuffing.

Preheat oven to 375°.

Heat olive oil in a large pan and sauté the garlic until it starts to turn golden. Mix in the tomatoes and add the basil. Raise heat. Add the wine when the mixture starts bubbling, and stir. Cover the pan, reduce heat, and simmer for 15 minutes. Adjust for salt and pepper.

Pour the sauce into a baking pan, then arrange the stuffed squid on top. Cover the pan tightly with foil and bake for 10 minutes. Remove the cover, baste gently (be careful not to break open the squid), and continue baking, uncovered, for 5 minutes.

Serve sprinkled with fresh parsley and garnished with lemon wedges.

Serves 4–6.

Stuffing for Squid
Ripeni per Calamari

You will need:

1 cup	coarse bread crumbs	2	slices hard salami, finely diced
½	small onion, minced	10	black olives, pitted and chopped
1	clove garlic, minced	1	egg, well beaten
1	hard-cooked egg, chopped	salt and pepper to taste	
2 tbsp	capers		

Preparation:

Combine all the stuffing ingredients in a bowl, along with the chopped-up fins and tentacles, and mix well. Stuff the hood of each squid at least ½ to ¾ full and pin closed with a toothpick. Set aside.

Baked Trout

Trote al Forno al Marsala

You will need:

4	trout (whole)	1 cup	bread crumbs
4 tbsp	extra virgin olive oil	2	lemons, each cut in half
2–3	cloves garlic, minced	½ cup	Marsala

handful fresh, chopped parsley

Preparation:

Heat olive oil in a skillet, then stir in the garlic and parsley. Mix in the bread crumbs, removing the pan from the heat when the crumbs begin to brown.

Preheat oven to 350°.

Clean the trout and pat it dry. Rub with two of the lemon halves, then place the fish side by side in an oiled baking pan. Sprinkle the bread crumbs over the trout, then sprinkle with juice from the other lemon.

Place the baking pan on the center rack and bake for 10 minutes (or a bit longer, depending upon size). Pour the Marsala over the fish and bake about 10 minutes longer, basting several times until done.

Serves 4.

Clams with Bread Crumbs
Vongole con Pangrattato

The clams need to be cleaned and set in water overnight in the refrigerator. Change the water once or twice. If any clams are dead (see note below), discard.

You will need:

12	cherrystone clams, cleaned and soaked	1	clove garlic, minced
1 cup	coarse bread crumbs	1 tsp	oregano
4 tbsp	extra virgin olive oil		juice of ½ lemon
1 tbsp	butter		salt and pepper to taste
handful fresh, finely chopped parsley			lemon wedges

Preparation:

Open the clams with a sharp knife, freeing the muscles from the shell. Discard the top shell, retaining the clam in the bottom shell. Save the juice. Set the clams aside.

Preheat oven to 425°.

Combine the clam juice and all the other ingredients except the lemon wedges. Divide this mixture into 12 equal parts, then spread each part over the clam in its shell.

Set the clams in a shallow pan and bake for 5 minutes, then brown them under the broiler.

Serve with lemon wedges.

Serves 4.

Variation: Another method is to mince all the clams into the mixture and add an egg. You can then fill both the top and bottom shells, the obvious advantage being that you end up with 24 instead of 12 servings.

Note: Tap a live clam and he will snap closed his shell. Any clam you can open without a struggle is either sick or dead.

Poultry

POLLAME

 AM DRIVEN TO point out that men have fared quite well with animals. All in all, our arrangements with dogs, cows, horses, and even goats have been reasonably friendly. When it comes to fish, our association has at least been equitable. Any fisherman will admit to feeding bait to his intended dinner for hours before the fish agrees that turnabout is fair play, finally allowing himself to feed the fisherman.

Domesticated fowl, on the other hand, is a different matter, indeed. There is some intrinsic flaw in a bird that makes him admirable in flight but despicable in captivity. No one can truly know a goose without hating him. And the chicken is the sociopath of the barnyard. If a wild bird can be beautiful, even magnificent, a chicken can be neither and is without expectations for improvement. My most charitable description: a smelly, vindictive tyrant whose only saving grace is that he tastes good.

Chicken and Fish
POLLO E PESCE

It would appear that chicken will blend with nearly any other food. To demonstrate this, I suggest you try the following, which mixes bird and fish. You will note that only the breast of the chicken is used. You need not despair that you will have the rest of the chicken on your hands forever, since I also recommend you try the recipe for Pollo Fra Diavolo (page 164), which puts the rest to good use.

You know, many books on cooking are not so considerate of their readers and often leave them with various chicken parts unused and lying around the kitchen. This book does not do this. It is permitted that you admit to your obvious wisdom in choosing it.

You will need:

I	large boneless chicken breast, skinned and sliced into strips	3 tbsp	butter
I lb	fish fillets (sole, perch, or the like), sliced into strips	4 tbsp	extra virgin olive oil
I	lemon	I	clove garlic, sliced
all-purpose flour (for dredging)		½ cup	Marsala
salt and pepper to taste		12	dried figs (optional)
		lemon wedges	

Preparation:

Rub chicken and fish with lemon, dredge in flour, and sprinkle with salt and pepper. Melt butter in a skillet and add olive oil and garlic. Add the strips of chicken and fish before the butter browns. Sauté a few minutes on each side, turning only once. Remove chicken and fish, set them aside, and keep warm.

Pour off excess fat from pan. Bring up heat and add the Marsala, stirring in the browned bits of flour. When liquid is reduced by half, return chicken and fish to pan. Baste with the Marsala, lower heat to a simmer, drop in the figs (if using), and cover pan. Simmer 3–5 minutes, and then serve with lemon wedges.

Serves 3–4.

Brother Devil's Chicken
POLLO FRA DIAVOLO

The last recipe used only the chicken breast, so, as promised, here is one that uses the rest of the bird. With this dish, you will have to skin the chicken parts and marinate them for an hour or so. You will need a sharp knife.

Have I mentioned this need before? Truly, if you do not have a sharp knife, I recommend you take your family to a restaurant. Little can be done without a sharp knife except discover the need for one.

Buy for yourself a long steel knife-sharpener. It is expensive, naturally, and you will therefore take good care of it. It will be a thing of beauty, and you will learn to slice downward with the knife so that the blade shaves itself against the steel. It's all in the wrist.

The sound will bring your grandchildren's eyes to your activity, and they will consider you a man of magic and extraordinary powers. Think of spanning the generation gap with this simple device. They will learn, finally, that the old ways are the best ways.

Naturally, a good blade of carbon steel is best served by this great tool. Stainless steel looks good but does not take to sharpening very well. The use and care of your knives and the ceremony of their sharpening will become a legend with your family, and you will leave your descendants a patrimony in which they may take pride.

A good knife is better than a good tombstone.

Perhaps I should return to the chicken. You know, you really cannot place the blame upon me for these stray bits of advice. Had you a sharp knife to begin with, there would be no need to instruct you. I am aware that, being human, you will seek to place the blame elsewhere—that is, other than yourself. But since I am also human, I find this perfectly forgivable. Now, I insist upon getting to the chicken.

You will need:

chicken parts, excluding the breast,
   skinned (to equal about 3 lbs)
½ cup extra virgin olive oil
handful fresh, chopped basil leaves
salt and pepper to taste
all-purpose flour (for dredging)
3–4   cloves garlic, thinly sliced
1   sweet red onion, sliced
4   ripe plum tomatoes, peeled
   and chopped

2   sweet red peppers, skinned
   and cut in strips
½ cup sweet vermouth
1   dozen green olives, pitted
1 tsp   capers
½ tsp   cayenne pepper
juice of 1 lemon
handful fresh, chopped parsley

Preparation:

Marinate skinned chicken parts in olive oil, half the chopped basil, and salt and pepper. Leave for at least a few hours. (Do not discard marinade.)

Dredge chicken parts in flour. Heat marinade in a wide pan until fairly hot, and sauté chicken till browned. Remove chicken pieces, keeping them warm.

Add garlic and onion to pan and sauté for 5 minutes. Add tomatoes, breaking them with a fork, and then the remaining basil.

Simmer for 10 minutes, then add pepper strips and turn up heat. When mixture is bubbling briskly, add vermouth and cook 5 minutes over medium heat. Add olives, capers, and cayenne pepper. Taste for salt. Add chicken and any accumulated juices, return to boil, then immediately reduce heat. Cover pan and simmer until chicken is tender, about 10 minutes.

Sprinkle chicken with lemon juice, and toss some fresh, chopped parsley over each portion.

Serves 3–4.

Chicken with Lemon
POLLO AL LIMONE

This recipe has you marinate the chicken for several hours or overnight.

You will need:

1	4-lb chicken, cut into pieces	1	onion, finely chopped
grated zest of 1 lemon		2	cloves garlic, minced
juice of 1 lemon		1 tsp	rosemary
salt and pepper to taste		½ cup	Marsala
¼ cup	extra virgin olive oil, plus 2 tbsp	handful fresh, chopped parsley	

Preparation:

Make a marinade of lemon zest, lemon juice, ¼ cup olive oil, and salt and pepper. Mix well with the chicken parts and refrigerate for several hours or overnight.

Heat 2 tablespoons of olive oil in a large skillet, then add the onion, garlic, and rosemary. Add chicken pieces to pan and sauté until lightly browned. Raise heat to medium high and add Marsala. When liquid starts to bubble, cover pan and reduce heat to a low simmer. Continue to cook slowly until chicken is tender, about 15–20 minutes.

Remove from heat, taste for salt and pepper, and sprinkle with chopped parsley.

Serves 4–6.

 **Chicken Royale**

Pollo alla Reale

This dish goes well with rice or buttered noodles.

You will need:

I	frying chicken, washed and cut up	I tsp	oregano
	all-purpose flour (for dredging)	½ tsp	thyme
	salt and pepper to taste	½ tsp	tarragon
¾ cup	vegetable oil	½ cup	Chicken Broth, or more (see page 66)
I	onion, diced	¼ lb	mushrooms, sliced
I	green bell pepper, diced		

Preparation:

Dredge chicken in flour and sprinkle with salt and pepper. Heat oil in a large pan until hot and flash fry chicken parts until golden brown. Remove from pan, set aside, and keep warm.

Reserve 4 tablespoons of oil from the pan, discarding any sediment. Sauté onion in the oil; when translucent, add bell pepper, oregano, thyme, and tarragon. Simmer and stir 5 minutes. Add chicken broth and bring to a boil. Return chicken to pan and spoon juices over the pieces.

Simmer, covered, for 15 minutes, turning chicken after about 7 or 8 minutes. Add mushrooms and salt and pepper. Add more broth if mixture is too dry. (Remember, the mushrooms will throw out juice.) Cover and simmer 5 minutes more.

Serves 4–6.

Baked Chicken Pizzaiola
Pollo Arrosto alla Pizzaiola

You will need:

I	3–4-lb fryer chicken, cut up	5–6	fresh, chopped basil leaves
all-purpose flour (for dredging)		I tsp	oregano
salt and pepper to taste		½ lb	mozzarella cheese, shredded
½ cup	extra virgin olive oil	grated Romano cheese	
2–3	cloves garlic, sliced		
I ½ lbs	plum tomatoes, peeled and chopped (or one 28 oz can crushed tomatoes)		

Preparation:

Preheat oven to 375°.

Dredge chicken in flour and sprinkle with salt and pepper. Heat olive oil in a large skillet, brown the chicken, and then remove, keeping the pieces warm. Drain off some oil—but not the sediment—leaving about ¼ cup in the pan. Add garlic and then tomatoes. Cook at a fast simmer, uncovered, for 10 minutes. Break up tomatoes, add the basil and oregano, and adjust for salt while the mixture cooks.

Spoon some of the sauce onto the bottom of a baking dish. Arrange chicken pieces on top. Sprinkle mozzarella over chicken, then cover with remaining sauce. Sprinkle grated Romano cheese over sauce, cover pan tightly with foil, and bake for 20 minutes.

Remove the foil and bake 10 minutes longer. Let cool 5–10 minutes, so the cheeses will set.

Serves 3–4.

Chicken in Wine with Mushrooms and Peppers

Pollo Saltato al Vino con Funghi e Peperoni

You will need:

1	4-lb chicken, cut up		1 tsp	oregano
all-purpose flour (for dredging)			½ tsp	rosemary
salt and pepper to taste			2	green bell peppers, diced
½ cup	vegetable oil		handful fresh, chopped parsley	
4 tbsp	extra virgin olive oil		½ lb	mushrooms, sliced
3	cloves garlic, sliced		½ cup	dry white wine
1	onion, thinly sliced			

Preparation:

Dredge chicken in flour and sprinkle with salt and pepper. Heat vegetable oil in a large skillet and brown the pieces. Set aside.

Clean pan of the oil and sediment, then heat the olive oil in it and sauté garlic and onion. Add oregano and rosemary. Add diced peppers when onion is translucent. Stir and simmer 15 minutes. The peppers should be limp, but not quite cooked. Add parsley and salt and pepper.

Return chicken to pan, spooning sauce over it. Add the mushrooms, cover, and simmer for 3 minutes. Raise heat and add wine. Stir gently and cook for 5 minutes.

Remove from heat and allow pan to sit 5 minutes, covered, before serving.

Serves 4–6.

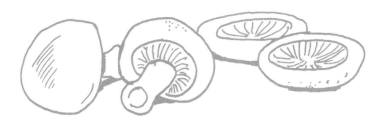

Baked Chicken and Eggplant
POLLO CON MELANZANE AL FORNO

You will need:

2 lbs	chicken pieces (thighs or breasts), skinned and boned	4	cloves garlic, sliced
salt		1 can	(28 oz) plum tomatoes
1	eggplant, peeled and sliced into ½″ slices	2 tbsp	oregano
½ cup	extra virgin olive oil	½ cup	fresh, chopped basil leaves
all-purpose flour (for dredging)		salt and pepper to taste	
		handful fresh, chopped parsley	

Preparation:

Sprinkle salt on eggplant slices and allow to drain for about an hour. Rinse and pat dry. Heat olive oil in skillet, flash fry the eggplant (do not discard any leftover oil), and transfer slices to paper towels.

Dredge chicken in flour, then slowly brown it in the eggplant pan, adding oil if necessary. Remove and keep warm.

Preheat oven to 350°.

Sauté garlic in the pan, adding more oil if needed, and add tomatoes, oregano, and basil. Break up tomatoes with a fork. Simmer 5 minutes, then adjust for salt and pepper. Return chicken to pan, then cover and simmer for 15 minutes.

Spread some of the tomato sauce in a heavy baking dish. Line bottom and sides with eggplant, creating an attractive pattern (overlap the slices slightly). Add the chicken and sauce. Cover and bake for 30 minutes. Remove from oven and allow to rest, uncovered, for 10 or 15 minutes.

When ready to serve, invert the baking dish onto a large serving platter so that the pattern of eggplant slices is on top. Garnish with fresh parsley.

Serves 4–6.

Sweet and Sour Chicken
Pollo Agrodolce

This recipe has you marinate the chicken overnight (or through the day).

You will need:

1	4-lb chicken, cut up		all-purpose flour (for dredging)
1 cup	Marsala		salt and pepper to taste
1	onion, minced	4 tbsp	extra virgin olive oil
2	whole cloves	1 cup	Chicken Broth (see page 66)
2	cloves garlic, sliced	2 tbsp	sugar
1	bay leaf	½ cup	white wine vinegar

Preparation:

For the marinade. Place chicken parts in a bowl. Heat Marsala, onion, cloves, garlic, and bay leaf in a saucepan and, just before the liquid boils, pour everything over the chicken. Cover and let cool. Refrigerate overnight or 8 hours.

Remove chicken parts from marinade. (Don't discard marinade.) Dredge pieces in flour and sprinkle with salt and pepper. Heat olive oil in a large skillet and sauté chicken for 5 minutes per side (until lightly browned) before removing from pan. Drain off most of the fat.

Discard bay leaf and cloves from marinade, then add marinade to the pan. Bring to a rolling boil for a few minutes, then return chicken to pan, spooning sauce over the pieces. Add broth and bring to a simmer, stirring occasionally. Cover and cook 15 minutes or until chicken pieces are tender, turning them at least once.

While chicken is simmering, heat sugar in a small saucepan until it melts to a golden color. Stir in vinegar. Pour sugar-vinegar mixture over chicken a few minutes before it is done, stirring to blend.

Serves 4–6.

Variation: Many Sicilians would advise you to drop in a handful of raisins and pine nuts with the vinegar. I have no argument with this—you may wish to try it. You understand, naturally, that we are addicted to these things and are prone to throw raisins and pine nuts into anything resembling a pot. Just a habit.

A Few More Words About Chicken

Now I wish to impart some further information about the thing that may stand you in good stead if you find yourself in trouble in the years to come. First, let us clear up what chickens are from the point of view of a butcher.

Age	Weight	Category
2–3 months	1½–2½ lbs	Broiler
3–5 months	2–3 lbs	Fryer
5–9 months	3–5 lbs	Roaster
7–10 months	over 4 lbs	Capon
10–12 months	over 3½ lbs	Fowl
over 12 months	over 3½ lbs	Old hen or rooster

You know, there are many, many more ways of handling chicken than have been touched upon here. Who has the time to list them all? You might consider the various recipes using fish and imagine substituting chicken for some of them. Also, chicken has a taste that will blend with most foods. Undoubtedly, the recipe for cioppino is a costly affair, but you can stretch it by adding chicken parts to the sauce first. It wouldn't be a true cioppino, but do you really care? And there is nothing done with veal that cannot be done with chicken at a fraction of the cost. Well, enough. I am impatient to leave this pernicious beast and get on to meats.

Beef, Lamb and Pork

Bue, Agnello, e Carne di Maiale

T IS PROBABLY UNFAIR to say that Sicilians don't eat much meat. This can probably be said of most people in the world. To be more accurate, Sicilians have never had as much meat as they would have liked. The results are, of course, the same. I mention it to explain why we have not expanded our skills in this area: a lack of opportunity, never of interest.

Much of the meat consumed is wild game, and I shall forgo getting too involved here, since such fare is not found in our supermarkets.

There is another thing, and it is of a delicate nature. When a Sicilian was presented an opportunity to use an animal for food, he took full advantage of it. Americans will, of course, eat some meat that is not muscle tissue, such as liver or kidneys. The Sicilian approach is much more serious. Not willing to overlook the slightest bit of protein, he makes use of everything from the glands and organs to the very marrow of the bones—and even the hooves!

Years ago, there were butcher shops that specialized in *sufrito*, or the "lights" (the innocuous English term for it). Here they sold everything except red meat. Such shops have long since gone. The younger people were impatient with the amount of work necessary to make *sufrito* presentable. Also, the government began to condemn some of the items—lungs, for instance—as illegal. *Sic transit gloria candidi.*

At any rate, I shall spare you most of the more primitive methods of attacking meat products. You obviously would have no chance to try them out, given the meddling of our government in private affairs. (And what is more private than what a man puts into his stomach?) Also, I am of the opinion that you would hesitate even if the opportunity came your way. I find this to be an embarrassing conversation.

Since I am speaking of embarrassing subjects, I might as well admit to a shameful thing. It is a long and dreary story, full of the best of intentions and the worst of conclusions. And since the facts have become fairly well known, I may as well admit my share of the blame.

You will have noticed that admitting to an obvious fault is often perceived to be a demonstration of moral integrity. If so, my admission will occasion only small loss and still make some profit in that direction. And so, the truth (though it cracks my teeth to say it): We Sicilians are probably responsible for French cooking!

I do not wish to make you uncomfortable, so I shall tell the tale hurriedly and touch upon only the main facts. Everyone knows that more than two

thousand years ago, Sicilian cooking was the model for all of Italy. Wherever the Roman army went, so went civilization (that is, Sicilian cooking). Well, the barbarian invasions put an end to civilization for a time, but Sicily remained the doorway to Italy; and through this portal, rice was introduced to the north and pasta to the south.

Now comes the sad part. Some years back, Catherine de' Medici, a northern lady of some reputation, married the French king and moved to the French court. Being familiar with their deplorable eating habits, she wisely brought with her an Italian kitchen: chefs, attendants, and the like. In this manner, Sicilian cooking—transplanted first to Florence—found its way over the Alps, only to be mongrelized through the subsequent centuries into what is today invidiously called haute cuisine.

I am saddened to have to repeat this tale, but now it is done. You are invited to make the most of it. Should you be seated one day at some outrageously expensive restaurant where they pour a tortured gravy over something's carcass, you will, no doubt, hold me at fault for your misery. I would only insist that my intentions were good and could not have anticipated this final disaster.

History, you know, is often such tawdry gossip, and by now you must be as tired of it as I. So let us discuss cooking, for there is more vitality in a small saucepan than in all the libraries of history.

Lemon Meat Loaf
POLPETTONE AL LIMONE

This simple stovetop meat loaf is equally good served hot or cold.

You will need:

2	slices stale bread		salt and pepper to taste
2	eggs, slightly beaten	¼ cup	Seasoned Bread Crumbs
3	lemons (2 for the sauce;		(see page 59)
	1, thinly sliced, for garnish)	4 tbsp	olive oil
2 lbs	lean beef, ground	1 tbsp	all-purpose flour
1 tbsp	fresh, chopped parsley		

Preparation:

Combine bread, eggs, and the juice of 1 lemon in a large bowl. Stir until the bread is soaked, then mix in the ground beef, parsley, and salt and pepper.

Shape the meat mixture into 2 oval loaves. Roll each loaf in the bread crumbs.

Heat olive oil in a large skillet and fry the loaves, turning them gently until they are browned on all sides. Stir the flour into ½ cup of cold water, adding it the hot skillet to form a thickened sauce. (Add a little more water if the sauce is too thick.)

Cook the loaves, covered, over medium heat for about 45 minutes, turning them occasionally and scraping the bottom of the skillet.

Remove the loaves, allowing them to rest about 10 minutes before slicing. Arrange the slices on a serving plate.

Add the juice of the other lemon to the skillet, bring up the heat, and stir the sauce, making sure to gather all the brown bits from the bottom of the pan. Pour over the sliced meat loaf and garnish the plate with lemon slices.

Serves 6.

Meat Loaf
Polpettone di Carne

With the addition of sausage, cheese, nuts, olives, and hard-cooked eggs, this is a meat loaf like no other.

You will need:

2 lbs	lean beef, ground	¼ lb	mozzarella cheese, cubed
I cup	Seasoned Bread Crumbs (see page 59)	¼ cup	pine nuts
		I0	black olives, pitted and sliced
2	eggs, well beaten	handful	fresh, chopped parsley
I	onion, minced	2	hard-cooked eggs, sliced
salt and pepper to taste		4 tbsp	extra virgin olive oil (plus additional for brushing)
½ lb	Italian sausage meat		
I tsp	oregano	½ cup	dry white wine (for basting)
I	clove garlic, minced		

Preparation:

Combine ground beef with bread crumbs, eggs, onion, and salt and pepper. Mix well and set aside.

Brown sausage meat in a skillet while adding salt and pepper, oregano, and garlic. Drain off the fat and let cool.

Preheat oven to 375°.

Take half the ground beef mixture and flatten it on the bottom of a baking pan. Spread cooled sausage on top. Mix together mozzarella cheese, pine nuts, olives, and parsley, and then spread mixture over the sausage. Arrange slices of hard-cooked eggs on top.

Shape the other half of the beef mixture into a shell that covers the sausage-cheese filling and blends into the bottom layer of ground beef. Brush the meat and the exposed insides of the pan with olive oil. Bake for 1 hour, basting with wine from time to time.

Remove meat loaf from pan and allow it to cool for 10 minutes before slicing.

Serves 4–8.

Skewered Rolls of Beef
Spiedini di Manzo

If you grill rather than fry these beef rolls, you will need three or four skewers. To prepare steaks, place between two sheets of waxed paper and pound gently with a wooden mallet until flattened and thin.

You will need:

6–8	thin steaks, pounded thin	1 cup	Seasoned Bread Crumbs (see page 59)
3 tbsp	extra virgin olive oil	¼ cup	extra virgin olive oil (if rolls are fried, not skewered)
1	large green pepper, diced small		
1	onion, chopped		

6–8 thin steaks, pounded thin
3 tbsp extra virgin olive oil
1 large green pepper, diced small
1 onion, chopped
3 cloves garlic, minced
½ tsp marjoram
salt and pepper to taste
1 tbsp capers
12 green olives, pitted and chopped
1 egg, well beaten

1 cup Seasoned Bread Crumbs (see page 59)
¼ cup extra virgin olive oil (if rolls are fried, not skewered)

Basting ingredients, if grilling

½ cup extra virgin olive oil
1 lemon
¼ cup fresh, chopped parsley
1 tsp oregano
salt and pepper to taste

Preparation:

Heat 3 tablespoons of olive oil in a large skillet. Add diced pepper, onion, garlic, marjoram, and salt and pepper. Stir and cover pan. Simmer 10 minutes, stirring occasionally until peppers are limp but not yet cooked. Add capers and stir. Remove from heat and set aside to cool.

Transfer mixture to a large bowl. Add olives and beaten egg and make a moist batter. Add bread crumbs, a little at a time, to form a firm filling.

Divide filling into as many portions as you have steaks. Spread each portion on a steak and roll up. Tie with twine.

You now have two options: skewering or frying.

Skewering. Skewer the rolls, two to a skewer, and grill them, basting with a sauce (see basting ingredients).

Frying. Heat the ¼ cup of olive oil in a skillet and flash fry the rolls so they are browned on all sides. Then treat them as you would meatballs or sausage, dropping them into a marinara sauce to have with pasta.

Either way you cannot go wrong.

Serves 6–8.

Beef Roll
Rotolo di Manzo

You will need:

1–1½ lbs	flank steak, pounded until very thin	handful fresh, coarsely chopped parsley
3	hard-cooked eggs, chopped	1 tsp oregano
½ cup	Seasoned Bread Crumbs (see page 59)	salt and pepper to taste
3	slices hard salami, minced fine	1 egg, well beaten
½	small onion, minced	4 tbsp extra virgin olive oil (plus additional for brushing)
1	clove garlic, minced	1 can (28 oz) plum tomatoes
10	black olives, pitted and sliced	4 tbsp dry white wine
1 tbsp	capers	½ lemon (optional)

Preparation:

Mix hard-cooked eggs with bread crumbs, salami, onion, garlic, olives, capers, parsley, oregano, and salt and pepper. Add beaten egg when mixture is well blended, then blend by hand. Add a little cold water if mixture is too dry.

Preheat oven to 375°.

Lay out the flank steak and spread the egg and salami mixture over it. Roll up carefully and tie with twine. Brush with olive oil. Sprinkle with salt and pepper.

Heat olive oil in a large skillet and brown the beef roll, turning every now and then so it browns on all sides. Transfer to a deep baking dish; set in the preheated oven.

Pour tomatoes into the hot skillet, then break them up with a fork. Season with salt and pepper, stirring to mix in the beef drippings. Simmer 10 minutes and then raise heat and add the wine, letting the sauce bubble briskly for 3–4 minutes.

Pour tomato sauce over the beef roll. Bake, uncovered, for 40–45 minutes, basting every 15 minutes. For added tang, squeeze some lemon onto the roll as you baste.

Remove from oven and let the beef roll sit at least 10 minutes before slicing.

Serves 4–6.

Note: Flank steak can be tough and is often too thick. One method for preparing it is to slice the thick portions sideways with a sharp knife—much like preparing veal cutlets. This will increase the surface of the meat even before you start to pound it.

Beefsteak and Bell Peppers

BISTECCA AI PEPERONI

You will need:

1 lb	top sirloin, cut into 2″ by ½″ strips		½ tsp	thyme
			salt and pepper to taste	
4 tbsp	extra virgin olive oil		2	large green bell peppers, sliced in strips
1	clove garlic, sliced			
1	large onion, sliced		½ tsp	celery salt
1 tsp	oregano			

Preparation:

Heat olive oil in a large skillet, then add garlic, onion, oregano, thyme, and salt and pepper. Stir and sauté for 3–4 minutes. Add beef and raise heat so that the meat fries rather than simmers. Stir occasionally and cook 10 minutes.

Stir in bell peppers and cook over medium heat, covered, for 10 minutes. Add celery salt and taste for seasonings. Continue cooking, stirring occasionally, until the peppers are done (about 5–10 minutes). Serve hot.

Serves 3–4.

Roast Leg of Lamb
Agnello al Forno

You will need:

1	small leg of lamb, about 3–5 lbs		juice of 1 lemon
2	cloves garlic, sliced	1 tsp	rosemary
4 tbsp	extra virgin olive oil	1 tsp	mint, crushed
grated zest of 1 lemon		salt and pepper to taste	

Preparation:

Preheat oven to 325°.

Wipe leg of lamb with a damp cloth. Cut random slits on the meaty side of the leg and insert slices of garlic.

To make the sauce, blend oil with all other ingredients in a small bowl.

Place lamb, meaty side up, in an oven pan and spoon sauce over it. Bake about 15 minutes per pound, basting frequently.

Allow lamb to rest for at least 15 minutes before slicing and serving.

Serves 4–5.

Baked Lamb's Head
Capozzella

The baking time is somewhat flexible to allow you enough time to consume some wine. I recommend you continue consuming the wine during the meal. Under no circumstances should you attempt to eat this dish cold. You will be very sorry if you fail to follow this advice.

There are sure to be fastidious souls who will object to this recipe, perhaps finding it indelicate. Without wishing to give offense we direct them to other, more "politically correct" cookbooks whose contents are more in keeping with their expectations.

We have pointed out that, concerning meat, Sicilians are serious people who have sought out ways to prepare the entire animal—even the hooves.

We do not care for hooves, but Capozzella is a fine dish whose appreciation takes only courage, and, again a little wine.

You will need:

1	lamb's head, in halves	salt and pepper to taste
½	lemon	3–4 cups white or red wine
½ tsp	oregano	(for drinking only)

Preparation:

Preheat oven to 350°.

Wash lamb's head halves thoroughly and pat dry. Rub outside of each half with lemon. Mix oregano and salt and pepper together and liberally sprinkle over each half.

Place both halves (eyes up) on a baking sheet. Bake for 35–40 minutes, more or less, and then serve hot with large chunks of warm Italian bread.

Serves 2.

 # *Liver and Onions with Mushrooms*
Fegato con Cipolle e Funghi

You will need:

1 ½ lbs liver (beef, calf, or lamb), carefully trimmed, sliced ¼″ thin
⅓ cup extra virgin olive oil
2 large onions, thinly sliced

½ cup all-purpose flour (for dredging)
salt and pepper to taste
¼ lb mushrooms, thinly sliced
½ cup Marsala

Preparation:

Heat olive oil in a large skillet and cook onions at low heat until translucent. Remove onions and set them aside.

Combine flour and salt in a bowl and coat the liver slices. Quickly brown the liver in skillet, turning once. Return onions to skillet, add mushrooms, and cook, covered, for 5 minutes at low heat. Remove cover, add wine, raise heat to high, and gently stir. The wine will bubble off; when it's half-evaporated, remove and serve the liver and vegetables.

Serves 4–6.

Sicilian Pork Sausage
SALSICCE DI MAIALE ALLA SICILIANA

You will need a meat grinder with a funnel piece at the end—but this is not really hard to find. Also, you will need sausage casings (salted), which are available in many meat markets. It only takes soaking the casings in warm water for a few hours and then rinsing them in tap water. A child could do it.

You will need:

5 lbs	lean pork (shoulder butt), cut in ½″ cubes	2 tbsp	fennel seeds
¼ cup	fresh, chopped parsley	2 tbsp	salt
2 tbsp	dried basil	1 tbsp	pepper
2 tbsp	oregano	1 tbsp	sugar
		1 cup	rosé wine

Preparation:

Combine all ingredients except wine in a large mixing bowl. (Make sure everything is extremely well blended.) Add wine. If mixture is still too dry to slide through the funnel, add cold water, a little at a time, until it is moist enough.

Slip end of the casing over the funnel and crank meat through. Every 5 inches or so, pinch meat and twist casing to form a link. Take care not to leave any air pockets in links.

Yields about 5 lbs.

Note: The wine will add to the flavor, but many people are not used to the taste. I assure you the sausage has not "gone bad"—it simply takes some getting used to. If you find it objectionable, simply leave it out.

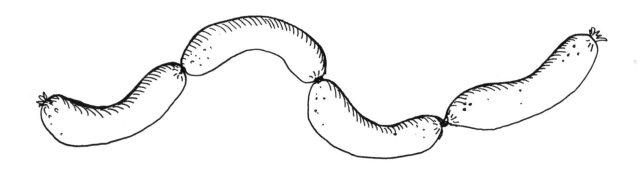

 **Baked Sausage, Palermo Style**

SALSICCE AL FORNO ALLA PALERMITANA

You will need:

2 lbs	sausage (links)		1 tsp	oregano
4 tbsp	extra virgin olive oil		¼ tsp	thyme
1 large	onion, thinly sliced		¼ tsp	celery salt
1 lb	green bell peppers, cut into strips		salt and pepper to taste	
1 lb	potatoes, cut bite-size		1 cup	Chicken Broth (see page 66)
			½ lb	mushrooms, quartered

Preparation:

Simmer sausages with 3 tablespoons of water in a large skillet. Flip after 5 minutes, add another 3 tablespoons of water, and continue simmering until water evaporates. Pierce links with a fork to release fat. Fry for 10 minutes, then flip and pierce again. Simmer 10 minutes more. Transfer sausages to a plate and drain fat from the pan. Preheat oven to 375°.

Heat olive oil in same pan. Add onion and sauté 5 minutes. Stir in bell peppers and sauté for 15 minutes more, stirring occasionally. Stir in potatoes, then add oregano, thyme, celery salt, salt and pepper, and ¼ cup of the broth. Replace broth a little at a time as it evaporates. Simmer 15–20 minutes, add mushrooms, and simmer another 5 minutes.

Set sausage links in a casserole dish with a cover, then arrange the vegetables on top of the meat. Bake, covered, for 20 minutes.

Let the casserole sit, uncovered, for 10 minutes before serving.

Serves 6–8.

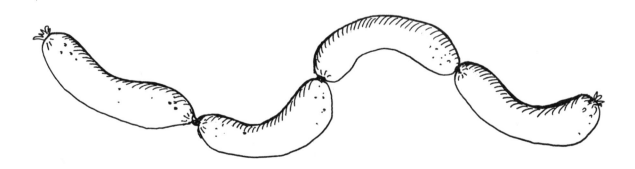

Pork Chops Pizzaiola
Costata di Maiale alla Pizzaiola

You will need:

6	center-cut pork chops, about 3 lbs in total
	all-purpose flour (for dusting)
1	egg, well beaten with 2 tbsp milk
1 cup	Seasoned Bread Crumbs (see page 59)
4 tbsp	extra virgin olive oil
2–3	cloves garlic, sliced

1 ½ lbs	plum tomatoes, peeled and chopped (or one 28 oz can crushed tomatoes)
1 tsp	oregano
	handful fresh, chopped basil leaves
	salt and pepper to taste
4 tbsp	dry white wine
¼ lb	mozzarella cheese, shredded
	grated Romano cheese

Preparation:

Dust pork chops with flour, dip them in egg mixture, and coat with seasoned bread crumbs. Bring olive oil to high heat and flash fry the chops for about 3 minutes on each side. Remove.

Lower the heat and add garlic to pan. Add tomatoes just before garlic browns, breaking them up with a fork. Simmer for 5 minutes, then add oregano, basil, and salt and pepper. Raise the heat to a fast bubble and add wine, cooking on high for 5 minutes.

Preheat oven to 400°. Coat bottom of a large ovenproof pan with some sauce and arrange the chops side by side. Spread mozzarella cheese evenly over chops, then spoon on remaining sauce. Sprinkle grated Romano cheese over sauce. Cover pan tightly with foil and bake for 30 minutes.

Allow to cool, uncovered, for 5 minutes.

Serves 4–6.

 # Veal
VITELLA

WITHOUT A DOUBT, veal is the most popular meat dish in Italy, and there are probably hundreds of ways of preparing the animal for the pot. Veal, in the south, is called *vitella* (heifer), because the male animals are used for work. In the north veal is vitello (calf), because the females are saved for producing milk and butter. But perhaps I am boring you with this pedantic stuff.

I was saying that there are so many ways to make this tasty dish that I hardly know where to begin. All recipes seem good, and each one is simpler than the last.

Come, I shall try to advise: you need only be sure that the veal is of good quality and sliced thinly. You cannot possibly fail.

Veal Scaloppine
Scaloppine di Vitella

You will need:

1 lb	veal, thinly sliced or cut into strips	4 tbsp	extra virgin olive oil
	all-purpose flour (for dusting)	½ cup	Marsala or dry vermouth
	salt and pepper to taste		juice of ½ lemon
4 tbsp	butter		handful fresh, chopped parsley

Preparation:

Dust veal with flour and sprinkle with salt and pepper. Heat butter and olive oil in saucepan. Sauté the veal, turning only once (about 1 minute per side). Remove from pan and keep warm.

Pour in wine and raise heat to a brisk boil. Cook 5 minutes. Stir in lemon juice. Return veal to pan and simmer until hot.

Serve garnished with fresh parsley.

Serves 3–4.

Variations: For additional lemon taste you might grate some of the zest into the sauce. You might even add mushrooms. All this is decoration. The recipe is so simple a child could succeed.

Note: The difference between the wines only determines whether you wish the taste to be sweet or dry.

Veal with Eggplant

SCALOPPINE DI VITELLA CON MELANZANE

You will need:

2	large eggplants, sliced, salted, and drained (see page 38 for preparation)	1 can	(28 oz) plum tomatoes, crushed
		1 tsp	oregano
extra virgin olive oil (at least ½ cup)			handful fresh, chopped basil leaves
6	boneless veal cutlets, thinly sliced and pounded (about 2½ lbs)		salt and pepper to taste
		4 tbsp	dry white wine
all-purpose flour (for dusting)		1 tbsp	capers
3	cloves garlic, sliced	10	green olives, pitted

Preparation:

Prepare eggplants, then heat olive oil and flash fry the slices at high heat, a few minutes on each side. (You may need more oil, depending upon the age of eggplant.) Remove eggplant and keep warm.

Dust veal cutlets with flour, then flash fry them at high heat, 2–3 minutes on each side. Transfer cutlets to a platter and keep warm.

Preheat oven to 375°.

Add garlic and tomatoes to pan (there should be about 4 tablespoons of oil remaining in pan). When tomatoes start bubbling briskly, add oregano, basil, and salt and pepper. Cook for 5 minutes at medium heat, then add wine.

Lower heat and simmer for 5 minutes. Stir in capers and olives, along with fried eggplant. Cover and simmer 5 minutes longer.

Arrange veal inside a shallow baking dish, then cover meat with eggplant and the sauce. Bake 5 minutes or longer. Serve hot.

Serves 6–8.

Note: The eggplant will absorb most of the oil. You may have enough to do the meat, but you will probably need to add more once you get to the tomatoes.

Skewered Veal Rolls
Spiedini di Vitella

For this recipe you will need four skewers.

You will need:

8	boneless veal cutlets, thinly sliced and pounded (about 3 lbs)	all-purpose flour (for dusting)
8	anchovy fillets, drained	salt and pepper to taste
¼ lb	mozzarella cheese, shredded	4 tbsp extra virgin olive oil
½ cup	fresh, chopped parsley	4 tbsp Marsala
½	onion, minced	4 tbsp Beef Broth (see page 66)

Preparation:

Preheat oven to 375°.

Spread out cutlets and, on each, place 1 anchovy plus an equal portion of mozzarella, parsley, and onion. Roll up each package and tie with twine. Dust each roll with flour and sprinkle with salt and pepper.

Heat olive oil in a large skillet and flash fry each roll, turning to brown evenly. Remove the rolls and allow to cool.

Pour Marsala into the hot skillet. Stir to blend in the drippings, and allow liquid to reduce by half. Stir in broth and remove from heat.

Thread two rolls on a skewer and place them in an ovenproof pan. Pour sauce over the rolls, cover tightly with foil, and bake for 30 minutes. Allow to cool 5 minutes before serving.

Serves 4–8.

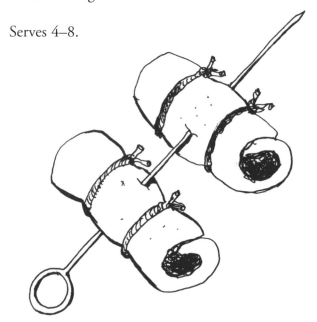

Veal Marsala

SCALOPPINE DI VITELLA AL MARSALA

You will need:

6	boneless veal cutlets, thinly sliced and pounded (about 2½ lbs)	½	small onion, minced
	all-purpose flour (for dusting)	¼ lb	mushrooms, thinly sliced
	salt and pepper to taste	4 tbsp	Marsala
4 tbsp	extra virgin olive oil	4 tbsp	Beef Broth (see page 66)
2	cloves garlic, minced	I	pinch nutmeg

Preparation:

Dust cutlets in flour and sprinkle with salt and pepper. Flash fry at high heat in olive oil for 2–3 minutes per side. Set aside and keep warm.

Heat olive oil in the same pan and sauté the garlic and onions until almost brown. Add mushrooms and simmer 3 minutes. Bring up heat and add Marsala and broth, stirring so the sediment from the pan blends into the sauce. Add nutmeg and salt and pepper.

Lower heat to a simmer and return the cutlets to the pan. Turn them once (so that both sides get the benefit of the sauce). Cover pan and allow to simmer 3–4 minutes before serving.

Serves 3–4.

Veal Cutlets Parmesan
Scaloppine di Vitella alla Parmigiana

You will need:

8	boneless veal cutlets, thinly sliced and pounded (about 3 lbs)	I can	(28 oz) plum tomatoes, crushed
	all-purpose flour (for dusting)	handful	fresh, chopped basil leaves
I	egg, well beaten with 2 tbsp milk	I tsp	oregano
I cup	Seasoned Bread Crumbs (see page 59)		salt and pepper to taste
		4 tbsp	dry white wine
4 tbsp	extra virgin olive oil	¼ lb	mozzarella cheese, shredded (about I cup)
2	cloves garlic, sliced	½ cup	grated Romano cheese

Preparation:

Preheat oven to 400°.

Dust cutlets with flour, dip in egg mixture, and coat with bread crumbs. Bring olive oil to high heat and flash fry cutlets, about 2–3 minutes per side. Set them aside and keep warm.

Lower heat. Add garlic to same pan and simmer, then add tomatoes and raise heat. When the tomatoes start bubbling, add basil, oregano, and salt and pepper, and continue cooking on medium heat about 10 minutes. Pour in wine and cook for another 3–5 minutes, stirring occasionally.

Spoon a layer of sauce into a large ovenproof pan, then place cutlets side by side. Spread mozzarella cheese over cutlets, then cover with remaining sauce. Top with grated Romano.

Cover pan with foil and bake for 30 minutes. Remove pan from oven, uncover, and allow to sit 5 minutes before serving.

Serves 4–6.

Pastry

Dolci

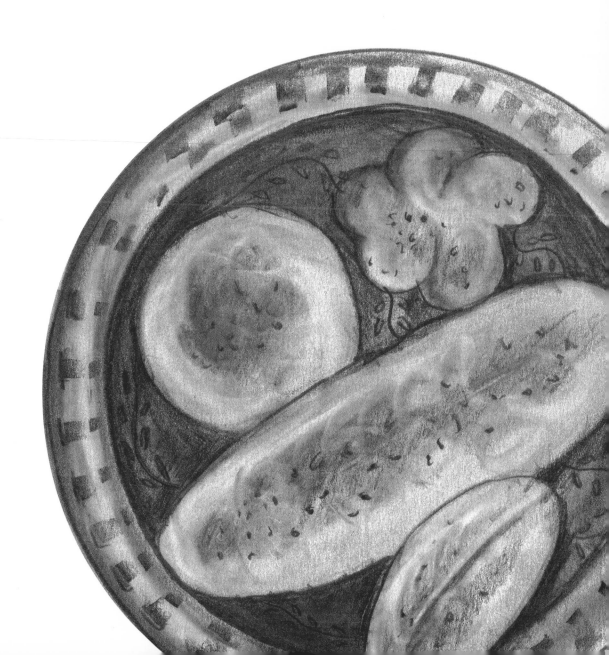

HE ARTFUL SURVIVOR in this world picks up what profit he finds in his path and adds it to the accumulated store in his tucker bag.* After a while, if he has been lucky, he is wealthy. The pastry of Sicily is just such a hoard of wealth, garnered in odd bits and pieces through the long centuries and added to with each successful invasion of our island. Some had much to give, some little more than nothing. But it all added up: a bit of Etruscan, a touch from of Greek, something from Carthage, something Roman. We even had Vikings here once. The French stay was cut short at Vespers, which was their own fault no matter what they say. After all, we accommodated everyone else without trouble.

"Scratch a Sicilian and find an Arab," runs the old saw, referring to the time when the Moors of Africa took up residence. A profitable stay, for we learned much from them about pastry. They like things sweet, you know. Drink tea with an Arab and you can dance a tarantella on the tea's surface, so thick it is with sugar.

So Sicilian pastry is very sweet and sometimes ornate and stuffed with cream and sweetened cheese and bits of fruit and candy. Of course, we added things that Arabs would avoid, such as alcohol. And would an Arab consider putting black pepper in a Christmas cookie? (Or more accurately for an Arab, would it be a cookie for the feast following Ramadan?) But we make a cookie packed with black pepper called fuccidati, and it is very tasty no matter what you are thinking.

Our Christmas things are our own. On the other hand, our Easter breads are as close to being Greek as we can get and still retain our decency.

Now, before you become annoyed with me about this, I wish to make clear that there is nothing really very wrong with being Greek. I have known quite a few Greeks, and aside from their habit of using too much sage and rosemary, and their curious addiction to oregano, I have found them quite sympathetic. It is only that their women are so formidable. Surely you must have noticed this. At one time, I seriously pondered why God decided to create Greek men, until I concluded it was done so as to afford someone to marry Greek women. Ah, but I am making too much of this.

Here, then, are some Sicilian pastry recipes. By no means is this collection complete, but I shall tell you what I remember. After all, it is better to have a few good ones than to fill many pages with lots of things about which I know nothing just to impress you with obscure erudition.

---

*A tucker bag is a tramp's knapsack, a term picked up from some Australian visitors a few years back. Australian cooking, by the way, is unfortunate.

Bread and Cake

I FIRST WISH TO CALL your attention to the wonder which occurs by heating some wet flour. You have surely noticed the magic of the thing. The wet flour puffs and grows and presents itself to us in golden majesty. Attend! I shall explain it.

There are three ways to make the magic work. The best is by using yeast, but that takes the longest. The second way is to use soda, the same bicarbonate that is used in hospitals for people suffering from an arrest. Here you must add an acid (such as buttermilk). The mix of acid and soda produces bubbles of gas which, in turn, puff up the flour. It is for this reason most recipes warn against too much mixing of the soda dough. It loses its puffiness with overhandling. The third way is by using baking powder. Here the gas is formed by the heat of the oven acting upon the chemical.

Yeast is best. It is not some interacting chemicals that make the magic. Yeast is alive and responds to the heat of your hands. You know, there are many people who have tried to make a yeast dough and who have been disappointed with the results and given up. But this is because they misunderstand what is happening. You must knead the dough! Truly, there is nothing you can do as important as kneading to encourage the yeast to do its best work.

I grant you that the shaggy mass of sticky dough seems hopeless when you first start to knead. Courage. Take heart and persevere. Rock with the dough, using your shoulders as well as your arms. Set up a soothing rhythm that will comfort the yeast into believing you know what you are about. And soon you will begin to believe it yourself.

Remember, if you do not knead properly and long enough, the magic will not work. And that is the end of the matter. Except … once you have finished kneading you should cover the dough and get it in a warm, quiet spot so the magic will work and the dough will grow. Be warned—this will take several hours. So be sure to plan ahead. Now, that truly ends the matter.

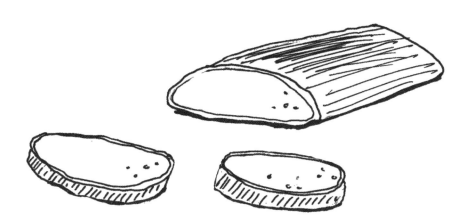

Raised Sweet Dough for Holiday Pastry
PASTA PER DOLCI PER LE FESTE

This is a yeast recipe, so recall what I have advised about properly kneading the dough. This particular dough is used for all kinds of sweet rolls and cakes. After rising, it is cut and formed into interesting fish and animal shapes with bits and sprinkles of multicolored candy on top. For this, it is best to roll out the dough first. Rolls or cake loaves may be shaped by hand and, naturally, take longer to bake.

You will need:

1 pkg	yeast		1 cup	sugar
9 oz	milk, lukewarm		4	eggs, well beaten
4 cups	all-purpose flour (plus additional for the board)		1 tsp	salt
			2 tsp	vanilla extract
½ cup	butter			

Preparation:

Dissolve yeast in warm milk, then combine with 1 cup flour in a large bowl. Blend and set in a warm place for 10–15 minutes.

Melt butter and combine in another bowl with sugar and eggs. Add salt, vanilla, and remaining flour. Finally, add yeast mixture. Mix well.

Place dough on a well-floured board and knead (courage!) until dough is smooth and elastic, adding a little more flour as required if dough is sticky. Cover with a dish towel and set in a warm place so it can double in size. This will take a few hours.

Place dough back on the floured board and punch down. You can now decide the sorts of shapes you wish for the dough. There are no rules here, so let your imagination soar. Once dough is shaped, set aside to rise again. (Place pieces a few inches apart on baking pan to allow for expansion.) Let the second rising be until the rolls are one-half again as large.

Preheat oven to 375°, then bake for about 25 minutes. Baking time will depend upon bulk, so it's best to check after 20 minutes.

Yields 6–8 sweet rolls or 1–2 cakes.

Sicilian Easter Bread

Pan di Pasqua alla Siciliana

The Easter bread of Sicily can be round, oblong, or doughnut-shaped, but it is nearly always braided and usually has colored hard-cooked eggs woven among the braids. Probably the most popular is the doughnut shape, which is a large loaf of great beauty studded with coral-colored eggs. We begin, though, with a simple Easter bread, which can be shaped into the form of your choosing.

You will need:

2 pkgs	yeast	3		eggs
½ cup	warm water	3		egg yolks (save whites for
I cup	sugar			brushing, if desired)
¾ cup	butter	⅔ cup		scalded milk (allowed to cool)
I tsp	salt	5–6 cups		all-purpose flour (plus extra
juice of I lemon				for the board)
grated zest of I lemon		milk and additional egg yolk (optional)		

Preparation:

Dissolve yeast in warm water and stir in a tablespoon of sugar. Set aside 10–15 minutes, until mixture froths.

Cream butter and remaining sugar in a large bowl, then add salt, lemon juice, and grated zest. Beat mixture until fluffy. Beat in whole eggs and yolks one at a time, then add cooled milk. Add frothy yeast mixture.

Add flour, one cup at a time, mixing until dough is stiff. Turn dough onto a floured board and knead, adding flour to keep from sticking, until dough is smooth and elastic (about 10–15 minutes). Place dough in a large buttered bowl, turning dough so its entire surface will be greased. Cover with a dish towel and set in a warm place. Allow dough to rise until double in bulk.

Punch dough down and knead again to remove bubbles. Shape dough into whatever form you choose and set aside, covered, to rise. (It will take less time now.)

Preheat oven to 325°. Bake for about 50 minutes. The length of time depends upon size and shape. It's a good idea to remove the loaf from the oven and tap its bottom. If the loaf doesn't sound hollow, return it to the oven and check again in 10 minutes.

Note: Brushing the dough with a mixture of egg white and a little water will give the crust a brown glaze. A deeper color will result with egg yolk and milk. If the crust looks too dark, you might cover the loaf with foil during the last 10–15 minutes of baking.

Yields 1 loaf of bread.

Sicilian Easter Ring

Ciambella Siciliana Pasquale

This is the very pretty traditional Easter bread. To create it, follow the instructions for Sicilian Easter Bread (page 201). Then, while the dough is rising, prepare the colored eggs. In addition to the Sicilian Easter Bread ingredients, you will need 5 hard-cooked eggs (unpeeled), food coloring, and a couple of egg whites.

Preparation:

Preheat oven to 325°.

Color the hard-cooked eggs. A variety of colors is traditional—red (or deep rose), blue, violet, yellow … or any other bright shade.

The dye is going to slightly discolor the bread baked around the eggs. Though you can't eliminate it completely, there is a way to minimize the discoloration. After dying the eggs, brush on a coating of egg white, and then heat the eggs in a low oven until coating dries (check after 3 minutes). (You may want to use several coatings; just make sure each one is dry before you apply the next.)

When the dough has risen and been punched down, separate it into three equal parts.

Roll each part to form a rope about 30 inches long. Place the ropes on a large, greased baking dish. You must braid the ropes loosely without pulling or stretching them. Curve the braid into a circle. At five evenly spaced intervals, gently separate the strands to accommodate a colored egg (pointed side down). Arrange the strands to form a cup for holding an egg in place; then close up by pinching the ropes together tightly and forming a good seal with an egg white.

Bake for about 50 minutes, then set the ring on a cooling rack for at least 15 minutes before slicing.

The Easter ring may be served warm or cool.

Yields one 2-lb Easter ring.

 # *Christmas Bread*
PANETTONE

Actually, panettone is a northern invention. However, it is so closely associated with Christmas that you will find it on all Italian tables during the holiday season.

You will need:

I pkg	yeast		I tbsp	orange extract
4 tbsp	warm water		I tbsp	vanilla extract
½ cup	melted butter		I tbsp	anise extract (or Sambuca)
⅔ cup	sugar		I tbsp	anise seeds
½ tsp	salt		I tsp	grated lemon zest
¾ cup	milk, scalded and cooled		¼ cup	each pine nuts, raisins, and
3½	cups all-purpose flour			chopped candied fruit
3	eggs, well beaten			

Preparation:

Use a small bowl, and dissolve yeast in warm water. Let stand until frothy (about 10 minutes).

In a separate bowl, mix butter, sugar, and salt. Add half the milk and ½ cup flour. Blend until smooth. Add remaining milk and another ½ cup of flour. Work batter until smooth.

Add beaten eggs to dissolved yeast, along with extracts, anise seeds, and lemon zest. Pour this mixture into batter and blend well. Add remaining flour gradually, forming a stiff dough. Knead dough on a floured board until smooth and elastic, then form it into a ball. Transfer to a large buttered bowl, turning dough once so its entire surface is greased. Cover bowl with a dish towel, allowing dough to rise until triple in size. This will take several hours.

Preheat oven to 350°.

Punch dough down and turn it onto a floured board. Fold in the nuts, raisins, and candied fruit as you knead, making sure they are well distributed. Form into a ball, then place it inside a buttered brown paper bag, spring form, or coffee can. (See Note, below.) Bake for 45–55 minutes, or until bread is well-browned and tests clean at the center.

Remove from oven, then wrap loosely—both the loaf and the receptacle—in a clean cloth and then in foil. Allow to cool slowly. (When the loaf has cooled completely, it will be liberated from the receptacle.)

Yields one 1½-lb panettone.

Note: A #6 brown paper bag (an ordinary lunch bag) is a perfect size. The height works just fine. Simply open up, then fold down the top to form a 2½″ cuff. You can also use a spring form (bottom in place), or even a 3-pound coffee can. When the loaf is cool, you tear away the paper; unhook the spring of the spring form; or remove the bottom lid of the can with an opener, slide a sharp thin knife around the sides, and pop the panettone out of the can by pushing from the bottom.

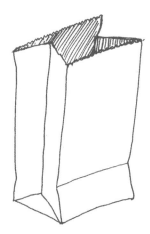

Sponge Cake
PAN DI SPAGNA

You can bake this cake in either a spring-form (tube) or a standard cake pan.

You will need:

I cup	sugar		I tsp	baking powder
5	eggs, separated		½ tsp	salt
2 tbsp	lemon juice		I cup	sifted cake flour
I tbsp	vanilla extract			

Preparation:

Preheat oven to 325°.

In a large mixing bowl, combine ½ cup of the sugar with the egg yolks, lemon juice, vanilla extract, and baking powder. Beat until thick, then set aside.

In a separate bowl, beat (high speed) egg whites with salt until frothy. Gradually add remaining sugar and beat until peaks are formed. Gently fold the egg yolk mixture into the beaten whites. Fold in flour, a little at a time, until you have a smooth batter.

Bake for 60 minutes if you are using a spring-form (tube) pan. If using a standard pan, bake for about 50 minutes. Test with a knife blade inserted into the center, and remove from oven when knife comes out clean. Allow to set 5 minutes before transferring to a cooling rack. Remove from pan when cake is completely cool.

Yields one 10-inch, ½-lb sponge cake.

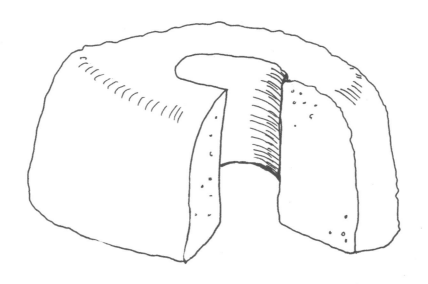

Cream-Filled Cake
CASSATA

Cassata is a Sicilian cream-filled, chocolate frosted cake, so rich and thick that only with great difficulty may one determine where cream leaves off and cake begins. It is theoretically possible to achieve a case of gout merely by glancing at a slice. It is definitely not recommended for diabetics. However, if you have a heroic stomach and an insatiable sweet tooth, you may wish to inquire further. To make the effort a little easier, you can start off with a good store-bought pound cake. Remember that you should assemble the cake a good day in advance.

You will need:

For the cake

1	fresh pound cake (about 4″ by 10″)
2 lbs	ricotta cheese
2 tbsp	heavy cream
¼ cup	sugar
3 tbsp	Triple Sec (or other orange-based liqueur)
3 tbsp	mixed candied fruit, coarsely chopped

2 oz	semisweet chocolate, coarsely chopped

For the frosting

12 oz	semisweet chocolate, chopped
4 tbsp	strong, black coffee
½ lb	sweet butter, cut into small pieces

Preparation:

Combine ricotta with cream, sugar, and liqueur, and mix until smooth. Fold in candied fruit and chocolate with a spatula.

With a sharp knife, cut off ends of cake and level off the top. Slice cake into horizontal slabs about ½″ thick or less. (You should have 6–8 slabs.) Center the bottom slab on a plate and generously spread on the ricotta mixture. Top with the second slab, and again spread the mixture generously. Keep all sides flush and continue layering and spreading, until you have reassembled the entire cake. Chill at least 2 hours for the ricotta to become firm, then add the frosting.

Frosting. Melt the chocolate into the coffee, then remove from heat. Stir in the butter and blend, a little at a time, until smooth. Allow to cool until frosting is thick enough to spread over chilled cake. Using a spatula, spread frosting on top and sides, swirling it decoratively. You may wish to use a pastry tube to create designs and flower buds.

Refrigerate cake at least a full day before serving.

Serves about 10, more or less. Insulin injections are optional.

Cannoli

I cannot believe there might be some who do not know what a cannoli is, but I shall take it upon faith that it is possible. A cannoli is a crusty tube of flaky dough into which is stuffed a creamy sweet cheese. This recipe will yield 8–10 cannoli tubes. (I still don't believe it.)

I have been reminded that rolling out the dough can be tedious and frustrating. If you are fortunate enough to have a pasta machine, you can achieve the feat without the labor.

You will need:

For the pastry

2 cups	all-purpose flour
⅓ cup	sugar
½ tsp	salt
3 tbsp	melted butter
2	eggs, well beaten
4 tbsp	dry white wine or Marsala
2 tbsp	brandy extract
vegetable oil for deep frying	
(approximately 4 cups)	
egg white (for sealing)	

For the filling

2 lbs	ricotta cheese
1 ½ cups	sugar
2 tsp	vanilla extract
2½ tsp	orange flower water*
½ cup	candied citron, finely chopped
¼ cup	semisweet chocolate bits

For the topping

blanched pistachio nuts, finely chopped	
½ cup	powdered sugar

Preparation:

Pastry. You will need 6 wooden dowels, or aluminum tubes, about ⅞″ in diameter and 5–6″ long.** You'll also need a deep-fryer or a deep pan, since you'll be frying the dough in 3″ of oil. (The larger the pan, the more tubes it can hold.)

Combine flour, sugar, salt, butter, and eggs in a large mixing bowl. Stir and blend in wine and brandy extract, a little at a time, until dough holds together. If too dry, add more wine. Knead into a ball and refrigerate for ½ hour.

To cut dough, you will need an oval shape about 5½″ long. A 2-pound coffee can will work. The can will cut a circle, and you can use a rolling pin to elongate the dough into an oval.

Heat oil to 375°.

Remove dough from refrigerator and cut in half. Roll out first half on a floured board to a ¹⁄₁₆″ thickness. Cut as many circles as you can from one rolling. Add leftover bits of dough to the other half, and repeat the process. Roll each circle into an oval.

Lay a dowel across an oval and fold over to form a tube. Seal with an egg white. Drop tubes (including the dowel) into the hot oil as you make them. When tubes are golden brown, remove and cool on paper towels. When cool, carefully slip off the dowel. Reuse the dowel on the next oval.

Stuff tubes with filling, and sprinkle with powdered sugar.

Filling. Combine all the filling ingredients in a mixing bowl, whipping them into a smooth paste. Chill. Use a plain, large pastry tube to force the filling into each cannoli tube.

Topping. It is customary to garnish the cannoli ends with finely chopped, blanched pistachios and then sprinkle powdered sugar over the whole affair.

Makes 8–10 cannoli.

Variation: Some people, not satisfied to leave well enough alone, would have you garnish the ends with chopped chocolate or candied cherries, or both. There is such a thing as being too Arab. However, if your taste lies in that direction ...

Note: These things will not keep long. Only stuff as many as you plan to use that day. The tubes (unstuffed) can be stored for several days.

---

*available in specialty shops, large supermarkets, and Middle Eastern markets.
**available at restaurant supply shops and cake-decorating supply shops.

Cream Puffs
Zeppole alla Crema

The instructions are not going to sound right to you. Have faith.

You will need:

For the pastry		**For the cooked cream (crema)**	
1 cup	water	2	whole eggs
½ cup	butter, softened	2	egg yolks
2 tbsp	sugar	2 tsp	cornstarch
¼ tsp	salt	⅛ tsp	salt
1 cup	all-purpose flour	1 tsp	vanilla extract
1 tsp	vanilla extract	¾ cup	sugar
4	eggs	1 pint	light cream
powdered sugar (for sprinkling)		grated zest of 1 lemon	

Preparation:

Pastry. Preheat oven to 400°.

Combine water, butter, sugar, and salt in a saucepan and bring to a boil. Add flour all at once, and then vanilla. Stir vigorously until mixture forms a ball and leaves sides of pan. Remove from heat. Now add eggs, one at a time, beating briskly after each addition until you have a stiff dough.

Drop the dough by rounded spoonfuls onto a greased cookie sheet. Place them 1½–2″ apart. Bake 20–25 minutes. Remove from oven and cool puffs away from drafts (or they will collapse) before filling with the cooked cream.

Cooked cream. In a mixing bowl, combine whole eggs, egg yolks, cornstarch, salt, vanilla extract, and half the sugar. Beat together into a smooth consistency.

In a medium-size saucepan over low heat, dissolve the remaining sugar into the cream. When mixture reaches a slow boil, pour it gently into the mixing bowl containing the egg mixture. Beat contents with fast strokes.

Return entire mixture to the saucepan and cook, without letting it boil, until the cream thickens. Remove from heat and stir in lemon zest. Cool before chilling in the refrigerator.

Some words of warning: Do not freeze this cream. Also, do not let it sit in the refrigerator for more than a day or two. It is extremely delicate and susceptible to spoilage.

Stuffing the puffs. The best way to stuff is to slice the puffs in half horizontally. You will find the centers a little moist. Pluck out each center to make room for the cream. Gently push the halves back together (don't squeeze). Sprinkle with powdered sugar and serve chilled. Eat fast. They get damp overnight.

Makes 16–24 puffs.

Note: The crema is used in many other pastries. It is very often found in small tarts. These and other filled pastries are covered with a pie crust and baked. They are quite good.

Ricotta Pudding
BUDINO DI RICOTTA

You will need:

For the pudding

2 lbs	ricotta cheese
6 tbsp	almond paste
¼ cup	melted butter
4	egg yolks
½ cup	chopped glazed fruit
1 tsp	grated lemon zest
1 tsp	grated orange zest
1 oz	brandy
½ cup	all-purpose flour

½ tsp	cinnamon
¼ tsp	nutmeg
¾ cup	powdered sugar
4	egg whites

For the topping

½ pint	whipping cream
2 tsp	vanilla extract
¼ cup	powdered sugar

Preparation:

Preheat oven to 350°.

Mix the ricotta cheese, almond paste, butter, egg yolks, glazed fruit, grated lemon and orange zest, and brandy in a large bowl. Slowly add flour while continuing to mix. Add cinnamon, nutmeg, and ¾ cup of powdered sugar, blending well.

Beat egg whites until stiff, then gently fold them into the mixture.

Pour batter into a large mold or spring form (tube) and bake for 30 minutes. Test with a cold knife inserted into the center; it should come out clean.

Remove from oven and cool in mold or pan for 15–20 minutes. Slide out pudding as you invert it over a serving dish. Allow to cool completely.

Whip the cream with the vanilla extract and ¼ cup of powdered sugar, then spread the topping evenly over the pudding.

Serves 4–6.

Rice Pudding
Budino di Riso

You will need:

2 cups	cooked short-grain rice	1 tbsp	melted butter
2½ cups	milk	⅛ tsp	salt
½ cup	sugar		grated zest of 1 orange
½ cup	raisins	½ tsp	nutmeg
3	eggs, well beaten		

Preparation:

Use a glass baking dish approximately 8″ by 12″ and at least 2″ deep. Preheat oven to 375°.

Mix all ingredients, except the nutmeg, in baking dish. Sprinkle nutmeg over mixture and place baking dish in center of oven. Bake for 20 minutes. Remove and cool for 2 hours.

Serves 4–6.

Note: For this recipe, avoid using skim or partially skimmed milk.

Flaky Dough
PASTA FROLLA

Pasta frolla is a pie dough, but because it is unusually rich and tasty, it is also used for making filled cookies, crema-stuffed wonders, and cakes and tarts like crostate. This recipe will produce one 9″ covered pie or two 9″ open pies.

You will need:

½ cup	sugar		grated zest of 1 lemon
¼ lb	butter	3 tbsp	Marsala
3	egg yolks (retain whites for later use)	½ tsp	salt
		2 cups	all-purpose flour
1	whole egg		cold water

Preparation:

Cream sugar with butter in a large bowl, then blend in egg yolks, egg, lemon zest, and Marsala. In a separate bowl, mix salt into the flour. Gradually add the dry ingredients into the egg mixture.

Add whatever cold water is necessary, one spoonful at a time, to bind the dough. Roll into a ball and cover with waxed paper. Refrigerate at least an hour before use.

Makes 1 large tart or 2–3 small ones.

Note: Although this dough can be used for making many delicacies, it is usually treated as a pie dough and baked in a 350° oven. The retained egg whites are used to seal the pie or tart crusts.

Ricotta Pie
Torta di Ricotta

You will need:

1	recipe for Pasta Frolla (see opposite page)	2 oz	semisweet chocolate bits
2	eggs, well beaten	2 oz	chopped candied fruit
½ cup	sugar	2	egg whites
1 tsp	vanilla extract		powdered sugar (for sprinkling)
2 tbsp	orange flower water*	¼ cup	maraschino cherries, cut into halves
1 lb	ricotta cheese		

Preparation:

Follow the recipe for pasta frolla. Refrigerate while preparing the egg and cheese mixture. Preheat oven to 350°.

Combine eggs, granulated sugar, vanilla, and orange flower water and beat until frothy. Gradually beat in ricotta cheese and half the powdered sugar. Fold in chocolate and candied fruit. Set aside.

Roll out refrigerated dough on a floured board. Butter a 9″ pie pan. Roll dough to fit the pan, cutting off (and retaining) the excess bits.

Brush egg white on dough in the pan, and place in oven 3–5 minutes (so it won't get soggy). When the pastry is cool, pour in filling. Do not fill completely to the top. (The filling will expand and seep over during baking if too full.)

Make strips from the excess dough and create a checkerboard design on top of the pie. Seal with egg white.

Bake for 1¼ hours. Remove from oven and cool on a rack. Sprinkle powdered sugar over the pie, then decorate top with cherry halves. Cool completely and then refrigerate.

---

*available in specialty shops, large supermarkets, and Middle Eastern markets.

Fruit Tarts
CROSTATE

Crostate are tarts made with a Pasta Frolla dough. Usually they are simply filled with a fruit jam, such as cherry or plum. No doubt a commercial pie filling could be used to good effect.

You will need:

I	recipe for Pasta Frolla	I	egg white
	(see page 214)		colored candy bits (for sprinkling)
I	jar jam, more or less		

Preparation:

Follow the recipe for pasta frolla.

Preheat oven to 375°.

Divide dough into 2 balls, one large and one small. Roll the large ball to fit a pie pan or tart pans. The dough should be about ⅛″ thick. Place it in the pan(s) and then fill with jam.

Roll the small ball into a rectangle, then cut into ½″ strips. Lay the strips, lattice fashion, across the top of the filling. Brush dough with an egg white. Wind one extra-long strip around the inner edge of the pan to cover the edges.

Bake for 10 minutes, then reduce heat to 350°. Bake for 40 minutes or less, depending upon size of pastry. Cool and chill.

Makes 1 large tart or 2 or 3 small ones.

Note: If making small tarts, baking time can be reduced to 20–30 minutes.

Honey Balls

STRUFFOLI

This dish is also known as *pignolata*. It is decorative and tasty, and always sticky.

You will need:

2 cups	all-purpose flour (plus some additional)		2 tsp	anise extract
¾ cup	sugar		1	egg, well beaten
¼ tsp	salt		4–5 tbsp	cold water
1 tsp	baking powder		2 cups	vegetable oil
½ cup	melted butter		1 cup	honey
1 tsp	vanilla extract		2 tbsp	sugar
2 tsp	orange extract			colored candy bits (for sprinkling)

Preparation:

Combine flour, ¾ cup sugar, salt, and baking powder in a mixing bowl. In another bowl, mix butter, extracts, and egg. Pour butter and egg mixture into flour mixture. Mix well, adding a tablespoon of cold water at a time, until dough is stiff but not crumbly.

On a well-floured board, roll out dough to a thickness of ⅜″. Slice dough into strips ⅜″ wide, as many as you can. Cut strips into pieces ⅜″ long. Roll each piece into a little ball and set aside. Lightly flour the balls so they don't stick together.

Heat vegetable oil to 375° in a deep skillet. Fry the strips, rotating them so they achieve a uniform light brown color. Scoop them out with a strainer. Drain on paper towels.

Heat honey with 2 tablespoons of sugar and 2 tablespoons of water. The syrup should be liquidy. Immerse some of the balls into the honey mixture until they are coated, then place them in a strainer to drain off excess. (Reserve the drained-off honey.) Continue until all the balls are honey-coated.

Arrange the balls on a serving dish covered with a decorative paper. They should form a golden mound. Drizzle the remaining honey over them and sprinkle colored candy bits on top.

Makes about 2 lbs for about 20 servings.

Christmas Cookies
FUCCIDATI

Fuccidati is a fruit-filled Christmas cookie, and it is really called *Pasticceri di Natale, Ripiene di Frutta.* To make it easier, we call it fuccidati. There are many types of fillings for the cookies. I shall include three of them here.

   One interesting ingredient common to them all is black pepper. And why not? Columbus himself thought enough of black pepper to take a job with a gang of Spaniards. (Unhappily, though his trip was deemed successful, he came to a bad end. This is the usual result of working for foreigners. Look at Henry Hudson.)

You will need:

For the dough

I	recipe for Pasta Frolla (see page 214)
2 tsp	baking powder

Filling, recipe one

I lb	string figs, stems removed	½ tsp	black pepper
½ lb	pitted dates	¼ tsp	ground cloves
½ lb	pitted prunes	¼ tsp	cinnamon
½ lb	raisins	¼ tsp	nutmeg
½ lb	chopped candied fruit	4 tbsp	Marsala
¼ cup	candied orange peel	I	egg white
½ cup	chopped mixed nuts		colored candy bits (for sprinkling)

Filling, recipe two

I box	(12 oz) pitted prunes	¼ tsp	ground cloves
I box	(15 oz) seedless raisins	⅛ tsp	black pepper
	juice of I orange	4 oz	Marsala
	grated zest of I orange	I	egg white
¼ cup	sugar		colored candy bits (for sprinkling)
¼ tsp	nutmeg		

Filling, recipe three

2 lbs	pitted dates
1 lb	seedless raisins
½ lb	chopped mixed nuts
grated zest of 2 oranges	
½ tsp	nutmeg
¼ tsp	ground cloves

¼ tsp	cinnamon
¼ tsp	black pepper
½ cup	orange juice (or enough to make filling soft)
1	egg white
colored candy bits (for sprinkling)	

Preparation:

Add 2 teaspoons baking powder to the recipe for pasta frolla. Otherwise, follow instructions for dough and set aside.

Preheat oven to 375°.

Use a meat grinder or hand chopper for the filling. Grind the fruit, peel, nuts, and grated zest (according to recipe) into a mixing bowl. Add pepper and spices, sugar (recipe two), and Marsala or orange juice (recipe three). Mix well.

Use ¼ of the dough at a time. Roll to ⅛" on a sheet of waxed paper. Spread filling down the middle. Fold one side over the filling, then overlap the other side. Cut into 2" cookies.

Place cookies on well-greased cookie sheets, leaving an inch of space between. Brush tops of cookies with egg white and sprinkle with colored candy bits.

Bake 20–25 minutes or until cookies are golden brown. Remove and cool 10 minutes before transferring to a cooling rack.

Makes 2–3 dozen cookies.

Queen's (Sesame Seed) Biscuits
Biscotti della Regina

You will need:

2 cups	all-purpose flour	½ cup	butter
½ cup	sugar	1	egg, slightly beaten
⅛ tsp	salt	4 tbsp	milk
2 tsp	baking powder	½ cup	sesame seeds

Preparation:

Preheat oven to 375°.

Blend together in a large bowl the flour, sugar, salt, and baking powder. Add butter, cutting it in with a knife or cutter. Stir in egg; then stir in milk, a tablespoon at a time.

Divide the dough into four batches. On a well-floured board, roll each batch by hand until you have a long roll about ⅝″ in diameter. Cut it into pieces 2–3″ long. Roll each piece in sesame seeds so that all surfaces are coated.

Place the pieces on a well-greased cookie sheet, about ¾″ apart. Bake for about 15 minutes, until golden brown. Remove and cool 5 minutes before transferring to a cooling rack.

Makes 1½ dozen biscuits.

Anise Biscuits
BISCOTTI ALL'ANICE

You will need:

I	recipe for Sponge Cake (see page 206)	3 tsp	anise extract (replaces vanilla extract in the Sponge Cake recipe)

Preparation:

Follow the sponge cake recipe (but substitute anise extract for the vanilla extract). Preheat oven to 325°.

Set the dough on a well-greased cookie sheet. The dough should be about 5″ wide and at least 1″ high in the center (the sides will taper), running the length of the sheet.

Bake for 40 minutes or until golden brown. Remove from oven and allow to cool completely.

Slice the baked dough with a sharp knife into strips 1″ wide—each cookie will be about 1″ by 5″. Place the cookies on their sides on a cookie sheet and toast under the broiler 3–4 minutes. Turn and toast the other side. Remove and cool.

Makes 1 dozen biscuits.

Sicilian Crullers
Sfinghe

Sfinghe (pronounced sfinghe) is a kind of Sicilian cruller, except it is not made with yeast and it is not long and twisted. Otherwise, you might think it is a cruller.

You will need:

2 cups	all-purpose flour		½ cup	sugar
¼ tsp	salt		1 tbsp	light vegetable oil
3 tsp	baking powder		⅓ cup	milk
½ tsp	nutmeg			vegetable oil for frying (about 4 cups)
2	eggs			powdered sugar (for sprinkling)

Preparation:

Sift together the flour, salt, baking powder, and nutmeg. Beat together until smooth the eggs, sugar, tablespoon of vegetable oil, and milk. Blend the egg mixture into the flour mixture. Cover with a cloth and let stand about 15 minutes.

Heat the 4 cups of vegetable oil to 375° in deep fryer. Drop in the batter, a tablespoon at a time. Do not overcrowd. Cook until golden brown, about 5 minutes. Remove the sfinghe with a slotted spoon and drain them on paper towels. Cool on a rack and sprinkle with powdered sugar.

Makes 1½–2 dozen sfinghe.

GOOD SFINGHE, like good crullers, can be found in New York, but hardly anywhere else. They were popular during feast days in the Italian neighborhoods of Mulberry Street in lower Manhattan or the Arthur Avenue section of the Bronx. During those feasts (usually lasting about three days), the streets were sealed off to traffic and everybody walked or sat in folding chairs in the street. Young people flirted and old people gossiped, and there was also a big brass band (made up of men no less than 90 years of age) that played Rossini, Verdi, and Puccini. Sometimes the musicians even finished up together.

Every inch of street had food stalls selling freshly made wonders to the passing crowds: grilled sausages, peppers and veal, panelli, and sugar-dusted zeppole.

Everywhere you walked you could smell oregano, basil, and hot olive oil. It was a wonderful thing. Everybody ate.

Pan Crisps
PANELLI

Panelli is somewhat like polenta, except the flour used is made from ceci (garbanzos, or chick peas) instead of cornmeal. This is not a sweet biscuit, but you may grow to like it ... or not.

You will need:

1 cup	chickpea flour*		1 tsp	pepper
2 cups	water			handful fresh, chopped parsley
2 tsp	salt			

Preparation:

Combine flour and water and blend until smooth. Bring flour mixture to a boil over low heat, then add salt, pepper, and parsley. Stir constantly until the mixture thickens. Remove from heat and cool slightly.

Spread the batter onto a cookie sheet, using a spatula, until it is ½″ thick. Let cool completely. Cut into strips or squares, then either fry or bake them until crisp. (If baking, 375° for 20–25 minutes.)

Makes 1 dozen pan crisps.

CECI, ALSO CALLED CHICK peas or "garbanzos," are beans which, when cooked, go well with any kind of dish, including salads. They are even good when dried and eaten like a hard peanut. Indeed, the dried, salted ceci bean is combined with the fava bean (also dried) and commercially packaged as *"Fave e Ceci,"* which seems natural enough. Though very good, they have given the Planters' people little cause for concern.

Ceci, by the way, played a part in Italian history. When Garibaldi and his Redshirts fought the French, they used *"ceci"* as their password, since it is common knowledge that the French cannot pronounce the word. To be honest, I have never dared to test this theory on a Frenchman.

---

* available in some large supermarkets, Italian and East Indian shops, and health food stores.

Egg Wafers

PIZZELLE

Pizzelle are flat, dimpled cookies that go very well with a sweet wine or liqueur. They are similar to cialde—dimpled cookies that are rolled up like a scroll. Both types of cookies go well with sweet wine or liqueur. The ingredients are not the same, however, so the tastes are different. But if you have had enough sweet wine or liqueur, you may not really be able to tell the difference … except perhaps by the shape.

Both pizzelle and cialde are made by using the hinged baking irons that can be bought in most Italian grocery stores. Nowadays, there is even an electric model sold, so that Italian cookies can be turned out like waffles. But if making these the old-fashioned way, you really need to use a gas stove.

You will need:

3	eggs	1 tbsp	anise extract
¾ cup	sugar	1¾ cups	all-purpose flour
½ cup	melted butter	2 tsp	baking powder
½ tsp	grated lemon zest		

Preparation:

Beat eggs and gradually add sugar until mixture is smooth. Add butter, lemon zest, and anise extract.

Mix together the flour and baking powder, then gradually mix the dry ingredients into the egg mixture.

Place 1 tablespoon of batter in a hot baking iron and close the cover. Each wafer should cook for about ½ minute per side. (If you use the old-fashioned iron on a gas stove, heat the iron on a moderate flame, turning it occasionally to heat evenly. The iron should be hot enough to make a drop of water dance when it hits the surface.)

When the wafer is golden brown, lift from iron and place on a cooling rack.

Makes 2 dozen wafers.

Cruller Twists
ZEPPOLE

The dough for this recipe needs to chill for at least 2 hours.

You will need:

2 cups	all-purpose flour	4		eggs, well beaten
¼ cup	sugar	1 tbsp		grated orange zest
2 tsp	baking powder	2 tbsp		orange juice
½ tsp	salt	water (for the dough)		
⅛ tsp	cinnamon	vegetable oil for frying (about 4 cups)		
2 tbsp	melted butter	powdered sugar (for sprinkling)		

Preparation:

Combine flour, sugar, baking powder, salt, and cinnamon. Blend. Add melted butter and then the beaten eggs, orange zest, and orange juice. Add water, a tablespoonful at a time, to get a stiff dough.

Turn the dough onto a well-floured board and knead until smooth and elastic. Roll the dough into a ball, cover with waxed paper, and refrigerate for at least 2 hours.

Roll the dough out into a ⅛"-thick sheet. Cut into strips about ¾" wide and 6–8" long. Let stand about 15 minutes while the oil is heating.

Heat the vegetable oil to 375° in a deep fryer. Take each strip and give it a "double twist" before dropping into the hot oil. Do not crowd. Cook until golden brown, turning at least once. Drain on paper towels, then transfer to a cooling rack. Sprinkle with powdered sugar.

Makes 1 dozen zeppole.

Saint Joseph's Day Zeppole
Zeppole di San Giuseppe

In New York on Saint Patrick's Day, the Italians dress themselves in green and, with great knowing winks, pretend to be Irish. They march in the parade, even when it rains—and it usually does. Of course, two days later, on Saint Joseph's Day, the Irish are expected to reciprocate and eat themselves sick at the feasts. They usually do. Interestingly, the weather nearly always turns fair for the Italians. Perhaps they know something the Irish don't. At any rate, here is a pastry named after the event.

You will need:

1 pkg	yeast	½ tsp	cinnamon
1 cup	warm water	6 tbsp	melted butter
⅔ cup	sugar	4½ cups	all-purpose flour
2	eggs, well beaten		vegetable oil for frying (about 4 cups)
1 tsp	salt		powdered sugar (for sprinkling)

Preparation:

Dissolve yeast in ¼ cup of the warm water and let stand 10–15 minutes.

Combine sugar, eggs, salt, cinnamon, and melted butter in a bowl, along with the remaining ¾ cup of warm water. Beat in a cup of flour until smooth, then beat in the yeast mixture. Gradually add about 3 more cups of flour until the dough is stiff enough to knead.

Knead the dough on a well-floured board until smooth and elastic. Form into a ball, then place in an oiled bowl, turning once to grease the full surface. Cover and let rise in a warm place until double in bulk. Punch down and allow to rise a second time, until again double in bulk.

Roll out the dough to ¼″ thickness. Use an empty coffee can to cut 3″ circles from the dough. Place the circles onto a greased cookie sheet and cover, allowing the circles to rise for another 30 minutes. (The dough should be puffy.)

Meanwhile, heat the vegetable oil to 375° in a deep fryer. Drop circles of dough, one at a time, into the hot oil. Do not overcrowd. Cook until golden brown, turning once. Drain on paper towels and transfer to a serving dish. Sprinkle with powdered sugar.

Serve hot.

Makes 1 dozen zeppole.

The Song Ends

La Canzone e Finita

HEN WE WERE BOYS, long ago in New York, on feast days we'd huddle under the raised platform supporting the band shell and listen all afternoon as the old men played their best in honor of Puccini and Verdi. There we first heard the lovely "Intermezzo" from *Cavalleria Rusticana* and also *Turandot's* rousing "Nessun Dorma." In truth, they loved best "Señor Crescendo" (Rossini), and would stamp their feet above us as they played their hearts out. Such was our musical education—humble, but it sufficed.

Italian feasts, though now traditional in New York, were once unknown. Have I told you of the origin of these feasts? A Sicilian idea, naturally, and therefore touched with some small scandal. You will scarcely believe it.

A certain Sicilian, who shall remain nameless, owned a clam cellar at the lower end of Sullivan Street in Manhattan. He also owned a large papier-mâché figure of a saint, which he asserted to be St. Calogero, a Sicilian saint of questionable authenticity. The figure could be put together in sections and added to so that the finished form was extremely tall. At any rate, this dealer in clams would yearly proclaim a feast day and parade his saint the full length of the street, encouraging spectators to pin money "out of respect" on the passing figure. By the end of the feast the saint had reached enormous proportions—a full four stories high—and took a score of men to move. It was then retired to the clam cellar until the next year. The owner may even have contributed some of the money to charity. After all, the "poor box" at church is always open. Did I mention that he was reputed to be a member of the Black Hand?

St. Anthony's Church stands at the corner of Sullivan and Houston. Every year, the clerics condemned the entire affair and forbade the parishioners to attend, claiming that to do so would be sacrilegious. However, the shopkeepers found feasts to be good for business, and the people enjoyed the festivity. Finally, in desperation, the church announced its own feast day, March 19 (St. Giuseppe), and paraded its own saint. Competition was fierce for a while, but Giuseppe is, after all, the patron saint of all Italy. So Calogero was tucked away for good. For all I know, he may still be moldering in the nether regions of a certain ancient clam cellar.

I hope this story does not suggest that the Old Man was irreligious. He would even read the Bible upon occasion. His favorite story, naturally, was the one about loaves and fishes, where everybody ate.

 # A Final Word About the Old Man

WHAT I MOST enjoyed about the Old Man was his habit of deceiving the government whenever he got a chance to play a little "joke." He claimed it did not expect the truth and, furthermore, did not deserve it.

For example, some years back he took a trip to Europe with his wife. He was pushing seventy-nine at the time, didn't have a driver's license, and was in need of a ride to the passport office. I drove, and was therefore witness to his stories there. He started off by claiming that he was born in this country. I lacked the grace to blush, but managed to keep my mouth shut. I had long before learned that injecting truth into his conversations with others only led to confusion.

The officials asked for a copy of his birth certificate. I was willing to bet I would be surprised at the answer. The Old Man proclaimed that he was born in 1900 in the city of Boston and that, unfortunately, the city hall (and all records) had burned down that year.

Could he substantiate this? Of course he could, and he whipped out an official-looking document from Boston stating the city had no record of the Old Man's birth.

"You see. No available records. All burned in the fire," he proclaimed, smiling, and the bewildered officials promptly stamped his passport.

Later, I asked why he claimed Boston for a birthplace, since all our family is from New York. "Because New York's city hall didn't burn down in 1900."

So, for me, there has always been some doubt over the when and where of his birth. At least Boston has rejected the honor.

In 1916 he was with the army in Mexico chasing Pancho Villa, and the army seemed to think he was at least twenty years old. Possibly another little joke on the government. It must have been straightened out, because two years later, during the First World War, he would join the Navy. In the Second World War, he again would try for the Navy. But he ended up as an experimental-machinist working on the Manhattan Project. Now, how could he get top secret clearance without a birth certificate?

I do know the government and the country were two very separate things in his mind. He may have been proud when his sons volunteered for the Korean War, but he was careful to instruct them on what to report on income tax returns

One afternoon, I recall, we stood together fishing at a river. Out of curiosity, I asked him if he owned a license. He affirmed that he did. I was a little surprised. "You paid the state money for a license to fish?" I asked unbelievingly.

No, he explained. In this state they gave you one free if you were at least sixty-five years old. They probably thought at that age you could do no more harm.

I saw the license and pointed out to him that it gave him the right to catch scrapfish and bullfrogs. "So what?" was his reply.

"But we're fishing for trout," I reminded him.

He looked surprised. "They got trout in this river?"

"You know damn well they have trout in this river!"

"*Aspetta,* what do I know? I'm an old dago-man. I don't understand these things." And I swear to God his English started breaking down, turning into an old "Mustache Pete" Italian immigrant. And then he winked.

And this broken English coming out of a man who was once a radio announcer (April–May, 1927) for New York radio stations WJZ, WAAT, and WEAF.

What more I know about his life is from the stories he told: that he started working at twelve on the docks and railroads loading freight; that he was in two wars before he was eighteen; that he barnstormed an old "Jenny" in the early 1920s; that he tried near anything, including gunsmith, author, poet, mechanic, private investigator, electrician, watch repairman, radio announcer, and truant officer. He was even a cook.

Just before the Second World War he worked at the Hayden Planetarium at the American Museum of Natural History, lecturing school children on stars, constellations, and Greek and Roman mythology. He got the job by convincing the museum administration that his education included at least two years of college. (He never got past the 6th grade.)

The world simply did not frighten him. He was always cheerful and happy to be bustling about in it. Perhaps a gesture typical of this exuberance was that, in the middle of this nation's worst depression, the Old Man opened an employment agency in New York and came very close to making a success of it. (The failing factor? A partner who played the races.)

Mostly, I remember the warmth, love, and happiness of the home he created.

AND they were stronger hands than mine
That digged the Ruby from the earth—
More cunning brains that made it worth
The large desire of a king,
And stouter hearts that through the brine
Went down the perfect Pearl to bring.

Lo, I have wrought in common clay
Rude figures of a rough-hewn race,
Since pearls strew not the market-place
In this my town of banishment,
Where with the shifting dust I play,
And eat the bread of discontent.

Small mirth was in the making—now
I lift the cloth that cloaks the clay,
And, wearied, at thy feet I lay
My wares, ere I go forth to sell.
The long bazar will praise, but thou—
Heart of my heart—have I done well?

RUDYARD KIPLING

 # The Sicilian Gentleman on Wine

I HOPE YOU ARE NOT one of those wine aficionados who insist upon this nonsense about aging. Such people have always exasperated me. Long noses, pursed lips, and piggish little bellies. Pretending to know more than their fellows so as to think better of themselves.

A fine state of affairs, don't you think, when we cannot make our own wine without some governmental meddling. Well, that is the way of governments. They will have all our souls one day, much as they have our labor now. Don't allow me to get on the subject of government, please.

I was talking about wine. I have a theory about that. I firmly believe that all commercial wine is mass-produced in Hong Kong. I am convinced of this. You think not? Then why does it all taste the same? It has that grainy taste that betrays its source. Hong Kong, without a doubt.

My suspicion is that they ship it in bulk—possibly using second-hand oil tankers leased from Iran—to Sicily. I suppose they could just as well use Marseilles. In any event, the reason for the stopover is to color half the wine red. Sicilians probably add shoe polish or goat's liver. How should I know? God knows what those devils in Marseilles would use. Something that does not bear thinking about, obviously.

Next, they ship it to New Jersey. Why New Jersey? I can see you've never been there. Anything is possible in that swamp. There it is bottled, and a selection of labels is arbitrarily used to determine the prices charged. The finer the label, the higher the price. Some bottles are even dusted and rolled in cobwebs to correspond with the date on the label.

So, there you have it.

The only way to outwit these rascals is to make your own. Have some more wine. It cannot poison you, no matter the taste.

Epilogue

WE HAVE COME TO THE END. Since you have endured so far, you may as well grit your teeth and see this through. It may well be of some profit for you to do so, for I shall now tell you the Great Secret. Truly, the Secret of Secrets.

Sicilians have known it always and have clandestinely passed it down through the ages from a time even before the Romans.

It is this: all recipes are fraudulent, including the ones found here. They are hogwash, mere decoration to satisfy the onlooking world that the mechanical science of cooking can be contained in a written formula. Pure nonsense!

Cooking is not a science: it is an art. It is creative adventure, and the spirit of adventure cannot be contained in a recipe or a book, no matter the length.

When you have finally tired of beggaring yourself with buying cookbooks and clogging your numbed brain with their contents, you will begin to perceive that all those thousands of recipes are illusion. At best, they serve as mere whispered hints at direction.

Then you will begin to disregard all those petty and precisely written rules and pedantic instructions. You will, instead, finally determine to become a hero. You will march to the battlefield and, amid the clamor of pots and pans and the explosions of sauces and soufflés, will reach for glory with the inspired madness of a creative artist.

Remember, the world has never had enough of heroes, and a man should have a glory. Well, this is my last word on the subject. Fine art cannot be achieved by painting by numbers. But perhaps you have already suspected as much. If so, allow me to bring up something else.

It is sad news. The world is running short of Italians. Now, do not smile. I am in earnest. They keep migrating to unlikely places such as America, where they quickly acquire a foreign accent and a taste for strange foods. On the West Coast, for example, they eat pizza and strive to achieve a tan.

It would be completely unnecessary to argue the great need the world has for Italians. Even the French would concede this, and the French concede nothing, unless it profits them to do so.

I recommend that people be trained to become Italian. This only seems impossible, and furthermore, what alternative is there? Naturally, when I say "Italian" I refer to those people who live south of Palermo. Sicilians.

To become Sicilian, you must add thirty pounds and subtract three inches. It may be asked if the three inches are really necessary, particularly for people who are already short. To this I must ask, "Shorter than what?" It has been my observation that Sicilians are invariably three inches shorter than anyone else.

It may help if you train yourself to think short things. Perhaps you might practice stooping.

You must develop an interest in anything that is edible. Keep your eyes on the ground for treasures that others have passed by. There are, for example, tons of dandelion trod upon each year instead of being used in salads. If you live in the city surrounded by concrete, you will not have the advantage of rural areas where things push through the earth, begging to be eaten. Nevertheless, some gems may come your way. At the very least, it will help you in your stooping practice.

Ah, I see you grow bored with my chatter and are anxious to close. So be it. I am needed in the kitchen, anyway. Well, then, *la canzone e finita*. The song ends. And so do we.

Glossary

Glossary

A

Abbacchio.............................lamb
Aceto....................................vinegar
Affumicato..........................smoked
Aglio......................................garlic
Aglio e olio................garlic and oil
(a sauce or dip)
Agnello...................................lamb
Agrodolce.......................sweet/sour
Al dente..................................firm;
literally, "from the tooth"
Amaretto...............a sweet liqueur
(flavored with almonds)
Anace, anice..........................anise
Anguille.....................................eel
Anisette..............a colorless liqueur
(flavored with aniseed)
Antipasto..........................literally,
"before the meal"
Aragosta...............................lobster
Arancia.................................orange
Arancini................stuffed rice balls
Ardente...................hot, piquant
Arrostito.............................roasted
Arrosto...............................a roast
Asparagi.........................asparagus

B

Baccalà.............................salt cod

B (continued)

Bagno caldo.......................hot dip
Basilico....................................basil
Beccheria.................butcher's shop
Bigne..................................fritters
Bistecca.............................beefsteak
Braciolette..............small beef rolls
Bracioli.................stuffed beef rolls
Brodo...................................broth
Budino.............................pudding
Bue...............................beef (ox)
Buongustaio.....................gourmet

C

Cacciagione...............hunted game
Cacciatore..................hunter's style
Calamari...............................squid
Cannella..........................cinnamon
Cannellini.........white kidney beans
Cannoli...............filled pastry tubes
Capocollo.............a hot spiced ham
Caponatina, caponata.........eggplant
relish
Capozzella.....................lamb's head
Capperi.................................capers
Cappone..............................capon
Capretto...............kid (young goat)
Carciofi............................artichokes
Carduna..............................cardoon
Carne....................................meat
Cassaruola..........................casserole

Cassata.......cream-filled cake or tart
Cavolfiore.....................cauliflower
Cavolo................................cabbage
Ceci...................................chick peas
Cervelle.................................brains
Cialde....................................wafers
Ciambotte..................cabbage stew
Cioppino...................shellfish stew
Cipolle.................................onions
Coda...tail
Conserva..............preserve; purée
Contadino, contadina.........peasant
Contado.....................rural district
Cosciotto....................leg (lamb)
Costate...................cutlets, chops
Cotolette...............................cutlets
Cotta...................cooking, baking
Cozze...................................mussels
Crema....................................cream
Crocchette.....................croquettes
Crostate.........................pies, tarts
Crudo..raw
Cucina..................................kitchen

D

Dolce.......................................sweet
Dolci.....................sweets, pastries

E

Erbaserpentaria...................tarragon

F

Fagiolaio.........................bean eater
Fagioli, fagiuoli.....................beans
Fagiolini.....................French beans
Farcita...................stuffing, filling
Fegato......................................liver
Feste...................................holidays
Fico..fig
Filetto...................................fillet
Finocchio............................fennel
Formaggio.............................cheese
Forno.....................................bakey
Fra diavolo....................literally,
                          "of the devil"
Frittata..........an open-faced omelet
Frittelle...............................fritters
Fritto..fried
Frutta.......................................fruit
Frutti di mare........shellfish, seafood
Fuccidati.............Christmas cookies
Funghi.........................mushrooms

G

Gallina......................................hen
Gamberetti, gamberettini......shrimp
Garofani.................................cloves
Ghiotto..........................gluttonous
Ghiottone...........................gourmet
Granchio.................................crab
Griglia......................................grill

I

Imbottire..............................to stuff
Imbottita.............................stuffed

L

Lauro....................................bay leaf
Lenticchie.............................lentils
Limone.................................lemon

M

Macelleria..................butcher's shop
Maggiorana............sweet marjoram
Maiale..pork
Mandorle...........................almonds
Manzo.......................................beef
Marinara...........plain tomato sauce
Marinare.......................to marinate
Marsala.....................a rich brown
                              fortified wine
Melanzane.......................eggplants
Minestre.....................................soup
                          (generally thick)
Minestrina......................thin soup
Minestrone..........thick mixed soup
                               (vegetable)
Mozzarella...................a pure white
                        cheese, made from
                      buffalo's or cow's milk

N

Natala............................Christmas
Nocciole.............................filberts
Noce moscata.....................nutmeg
Noci...................................walnuts

O

Olio...oil
Olio di oliva ....olive oil
Olive.................................olives
Origano...........................oregano
Ostriche.............................oysters

P

Pancetta...............salt-cured pork
Pane......................................bread
Panelli...................fried ceci bread
Panettone........a spiced yeast bread
                          (for Christmas)
Pangrattato................bread crumbs
Panificio..............................bakery
Panino..........................bread roll
Panna....................................cream
Panna montata........whipped cream
Parmigiano....................Parmesan
            (a hard cow's-milk cheese)
Pasqua...............................Easter
Pasta asciutta.................dried pasta
Pasticcino.....................pastry shop
Pasticcio.................pie, pastry, cake

Pecorino...............ewe's-milk cheese
Peperoncini............dried red chilies
Peperoni.....................bell peppers
Pesce spada......................swordfish
Pesto..............................basil paste
Piccante.................spicy, piquant
Pigniolata (struffoli).......honey balls
(pastry)
Pignoli............................pine nuts
Piselli.....................................peas
Pizelle.....................anise wafers
Pizzaiola............baked with tomato
and cheese
Pizzelle...........................egg wafers
Polenta..............a type of cornmeal,
cooked into a cake
Polipi.................................octopus
Pollame............................poultry
Pollastra................................pullet
Pollo...............................chicken
Polpette.........................meatballs
Polpettine.................little meatballs
Pomodori........................tomatoes
Prezzemolo............................parsley
Primavera.....................springtime
Prosciutto.....................salt-cured,
air-dried pork
Provolone.......a straw-white cheese,
sometimes smoked

R

Ricotta............................a soft, mild
cheese
Ripieni..............................stuffed
Ripieno....................filling, stuffing
Riso..rice
Romano..................a hard Pecorino
cheese
Rosmarino........................rosemary
Rustico........................country style

S

Salsa....................................sauce
Salsiccia................................sausage
Salso......................................salt
Saltati................................sautéed
Salumerie.................sausage shops
Salvia.....................................sage
Sambucca............a colorless liqueur
(made from aniseed)
San Giuseppe...............Saint Joseph
(Saint Joseph's Day,
March 19th)
Sarde, sardelle....................sardines
Scaloppine...................thinly sliced
(meat)
Sedani.....................................celery
Seppie..............................cuttlefish

Sfinghe.............................a fried round pastry
Sogliole.............................sole
Spagna.............................sponge cake
Spalla.............................shoulder
Spinaci.............................spinach
Strega ....a bright yellow liqueur (made from herbs and flowers)
Stufato.............................stew
Sughi.............................sauces
Sugo di carne.................meat sauce

T

Tonna.............................tuna
Torta.............................tart
Triglie ....mullet
Trote.............................trout

U

Uccellette.................filled veal rolls
Umido.............................stew
Una festa.....................a saint's day
Uove.............................eggs
Uva.............................grapes

V

Verdure..................green vegetables
Vermouth..................a red or white aperitif (flavored with herbal extracts and spices)
Vitella.....................veal (heifer)
Vitello.....................veal (calf)
Vongole.....................clams

Z

Zafferano.............................saffron
Zenzero.............................ginger
Zeppole.....................a fried pastry
Zuppa.............................soup
Zuppare.................to make a soup; to moisten

Pasta Shapes

A LITTLE KNOWN fact is that among "traditional" Sicilians, mostaccioli and other short, tubular pastas were to be eaten only on Sunday. The long linguine or fettuccine were for the weekdays. There was an old-fashioned uncle who was shocked to sit at our table and find mostaccioli being served. It was not Sunday, but he ate anyway.

The list of pasta shapes—for weekdays or Sundays—is almost endless. Here's a sampling.

Cannelloni
Cannelloni, which means "big pipes," are long, large tubes. Make your own (page 96), then stuff them with a ricotta, meat, or vegetarian filling.

Capelli d'angelo (Angel hair)
Delicate and extremely thin, angel hair pasta takes only a couple of minutes to cook and is best suited to a light sauce. It works nicely in a dish like Crab alla Marinara (page 122)

Conghiglie (Shells)

Conghiglie, which are shaped like conch shells, are best stuffed and baked. You can fill them with ricotta cheese (page 106), meat, or vegetables.

Egg noodles

Make your own egg noodle dough (page 93). Add some chopped spinach for a green noodle, or pulverized beets for red.

Elbow macaroni

These curved tubes are suited for lots more than macaroni and cheese. They're perfect for Pasta e Fagioli (Pasta and Beans, page 130).

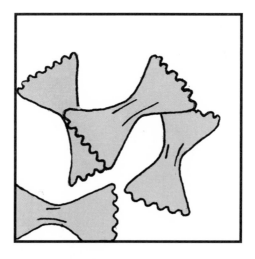

Farfalle (Bow ties, Butterflies)

This versatile and decorative pasta is often served with chunky sauces or in pasta salads. Some varieties of farfalle are egg free.

Fettuccine

"Little ribbons" is the literal meaning of fettuccine—flat, wide pasta strands that work well with both cream and tomato sauces. The most esteemed dish in the former group is Fettuccine all'Alfredo (page 113).

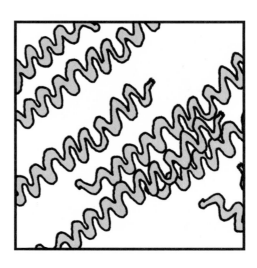

Fusilli

Fusilli—long and shaped like a corkscrew—is a versatile pasta that works well with hearty sauces or baked in a casserole.

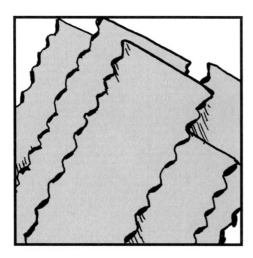

Lasagna

The name comes from the Latin for "cooking pot," and its edges may be flat or curly. It's almost always used in oven-baked entrées—meat, seafood, or vegetarian. Lasagna, Palermo Style (page 109) is a traditional recipe.

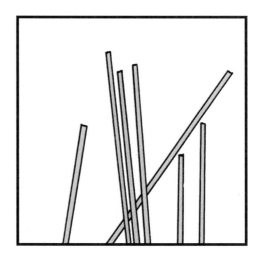

Linguine

Linguine, appropriately translated as "little tongues," are long, flat, and narrow—and just large enough for a red or white clam sauce (pages 118, 119).

Manicotti

From the Latin for "sleeves" or "little muffs," manicotti are excellent when you're entertaining. They can be stuffed and refrigerated (or frozen) for a later time (page 107).

Mostaccioli (Penne)

Whether you call them mostaccioli ("little mustaches) or penne ("quills"), these tubular shapes go well with tomato sauces (page 108) and almost everything else—including artichokes (page 129) and anchovies (page 116).

Ravioli

These pasta pillows (page 99) may be stuffed with beef, cheese, or vegetables. Variations include the half-moon-shaped agnolotti.

Rigatoni

Short, stubby pastas like rigatoni (meaning "large grooved") are good for holding creamy sauces or trapping meaty ones like a meat tomato sauce with ribs (page 105).

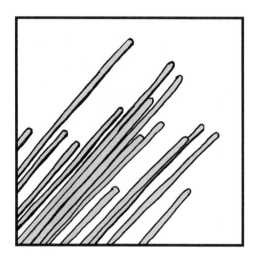

Spaghetti

Meaning "length of cord," spaghetti lends itself not only to basic tomato sauces, but also to those baked in casseroles. A thinner version, spaghettini, goes well in soup or lighter sauces, including an anchovy one (page 115).

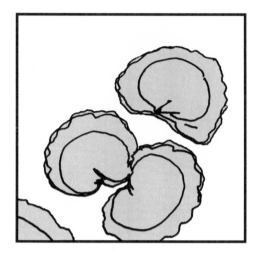

Tortellini

These small, ring-shaped twists of pasta may be filled with meat or cheese. Legend has it that they were inspired by the navel of the goddess Aphrodite.

Vermicelli

Long, rounded, and thinner than spaghetti, vermicelli ("little worms") are nicely suited to light sauces and soups.

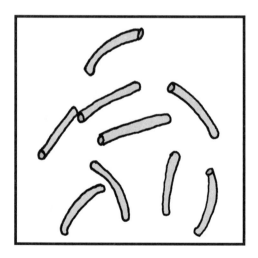

Ziti

Meaning "bridegrooms," ziti is often served at Sicilian weddings. Extremely versatile, it goes well with a variety of meat (page 105) or seafood sauces (pages 120, 121).

Conversion Tables

Metric Conversion Guide

	Metric	Imperial
Dry Measures	28 g	1 oz
	1 kg	2.2 lb
Liquid Measures	30 ml	1 fl oz
	250 ml	8 fl oz or 1 cup
Length	0.75 cm	¼ inch
	1.5 cm	½ inch
	2.5 cm	1 inch
Liquid and Volume Measures	5 ml	1 teaspoon
	15 ml	1 tablespoon
	1 litre	4¼ cups
Temperature	95ºC	200ºF
	120ºC	250ºF
	150ºC	300ºF
	165ºC	325ºF
	180ºC	350ºF
	190ºC	375ºF
	205ºC	400ºF
	230ºC	450ºF

Other Equivalents

	3 teaspoons	1 tablespoon
	4 tablespoons	¼ cup
	16 tablespoons	1 cup
Metric	1000 g	1 kg
	1000 ml	1 litre
	10 mm	1 cm
Imperial	16 oz	1 lb
	8 fl oz	1 cup
	16 fl oz	1 pint
	32 fl oz	1 quart

Index

Z